BACKROADS

— *from the* —

BELTWAY

BACKROADS
from the
BELTWAY

Your Guide to the Mid-Atlantic's Most Scenic Backroad Adventures

PAT AND CHUCK BLACKLEY

Voyageur Press

First published in 2007 by Voyageur Press, an imprint of MBI Publishing Company LLC, Galtier Plaza, Suite 200, 380 Jackson Street, St. Paul, MN 55101 USA

Voyageur Press titles are also available at discounts in bulk quantity for industrial or sales-promotional use. For details write to Special Sales Manager at MBI Publishing Company, Galtier Plaza, Suite 200, 380 Jackson Street, St. Paul, MN 55101 USA.

To find out more about our books, join us online at www.voyageurpress.com.

Editor: Josh Leventhal
Designer: Sara Holle
Maps by Mary Firth

Printed in China

Library of Congress Cataloging-in-Publication Data

Blackley, Pat.
  Backroads from the Beltway : your guide to the mid-Atlantic's most scenic backroad adventures / by Pat and Chuck Blackley.
    p. cm.
  Includes index.
  978-0-7603-2829-3 (softbound)
  1. Middle Atlantic States—Guidebooks. 2. Washington Region—Guidebooks. 3. Baltimore Region (Md.)—Guidebooks. 4. Scenic byways—Middle Atlantic States—Guidebooks. 5. Scenic byways—Washington Region—Guidebooks. 6. Scenic byways—Maryland—Baltimore Region—Guidebooks. 7. Automobile travel—Middle Atlantic States—Guidebooks. 8. Automobile travel—Washington Region—Guidebooks. 9. Automobile travel—Maryland—Baltimore Region—Guidebooks. I. Blackley, Chuck. II. Title.
  F106.B63 2007
  917.504'44—dc22
                    2007011529

On the front cover: Harpers Ferry, West Virginia, as seen from Maryland Heights.

On the back cover: (top) Shenandoah National Park and Skyline Drive from Little Stony Man. *(bottom left)* Schoolhouse at Ephrata, Pennsylvania, in spring. *(bottom right)* Sunset over Popes Creek, Maryland.

On the spine: Roddy Road Covered Bridge, Thurmont, Maryland.

On the title page: Bear Rocks Preserve, Dolly Sods Scenic Area, West Virginia. *(inset)* Autumn color on a backroad near Syria, Virginia.

CONTENTS

INTRODUCTION

ABOVE: *Trees are in full bloom for a springtime drive along Skyline Drive in Shenandoah National Park in Virginia.*

FACING PAGE: *Quiet country roads meander through Maryland's Montgomery County, such as this farm lane near Mount Ephraim.*

When we were asked to author a book to be titled *Backroads from the Beltway*, our first thought was "Hmmm. . . . Beltway. Backroads. That sounds like an oxymoron." The beltways referred to, after all, are those congested, multilane freeways encircling Washington, D.C. (the Capital Beltway) and Baltimore, Maryland (the Baltimore Beltway). These freeways service the Baltimore-Washington Metroplex, an area that also includes most of Northern Virginia and Central Maryland and is home to more than eight million people. In this densely populated Mid-Atlantic region, it is becoming increasingly difficult to find areas where one can escape the hubbub and get onto the true backroads.

However, while reviewing the volume of images in our stock photography files, we quickly realized that thousands of them, including many of our favorites, were taken along those very roads. The images reminded us that numerous possibilities for backroad adventures near the beltways do still exist.

So, we set out to re-travel and photograph our favorite backroads within a two-hundred-mile (more or less) radius of the Washington D.C./Baltimore Beltways, and we discovered many new roads along the way. The result is twenty-five trips within the states of Virginia, West Virginia, Maryland, Pennsylvania, Delaware, and New Jersey. The journeys were selected to offer a variety of scenery, historical attractions, recreational opportunities, and wildlife viewing.

For nature lovers, there are national, state, and regional parks, national forests, and wildlife refuges that boast an abundance of flora, fauna, and other natural wonders.

For history buffs, Colonial towns and plantations; presidential homes; forts and battlefields from the French and Indian, Revolutionary, and Civil Wars; historic churches and lighthouses; and canal towpaths and lock houses are just samplings of the historical attractions along these routes.

Outdoor recreation enthusiasts will find numerous chances to hike, bike, boat, fish, and swim. For those who enjoy camping, many locations offer pleasant campgrounds or primitive campsites.

The trips are also filled with opportunities for other pleasurable pursuits, such as antiquing, perusing eclectic shops and galleries, and dining in superb restaurants that feature regional specialties such as crab cakes or mountain trout.

The getaways vary in length. There are short jaunts that can easily be managed in a day, while other trips require two days or more to fully take advantage of all that the area has to offer.

Where appropriate, we suggest the best times to travel particular routes to catch calendar-specific spectacles such as wildflower blooms or migrations. We also identify areas where you might enjoy stunning sunrises or sunsets, locations for spotting wildlife, or hikes that are particularly rewarding.

Every effort has been made to keep you off major highways. While there may be faster, more direct routes to get you quickly from one stop to another, we focused on the most scenic, quieter backroads. We hope that the quiet character of these routes remains intact, despite the ever-increasing development in this heavily populated area of the country.

Don't embark on these treks without the necessities: hiking shoes, binoculars, and, of course, a camera. Bird and wildflower identification books might also add to the enjoyment of a trip. And, since backroads are rarely shown on state highway maps, a current state gazetteer or printout from an Internet mapping site will prove to be very helpful.

Most importantly, bring your sense of adventure. While we have pointed out interesting attractions along these routes, there are surely others that you might discover on your own. In this area of geological, historical, natural, and cultural diversity, a simple detour can lead to limitless rewards that await the curious and adventurous traveler.

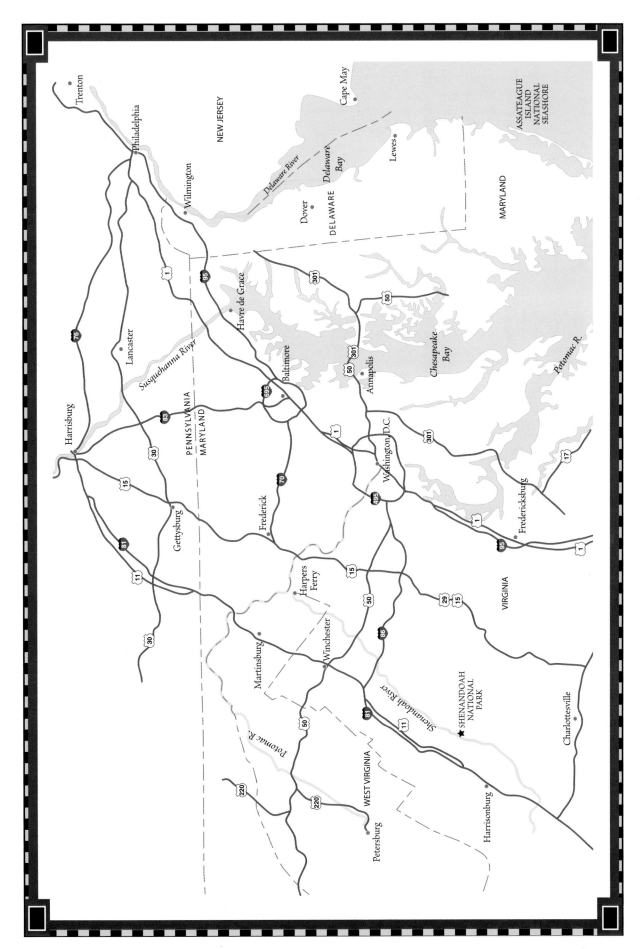

PART I

BLUE RIDGE LIVING

ABOVE: *Viewed from Shenandoah National Park's Skyline Drive, an early morning fog blankets the Browntown area in the Shenandoah Valley.*

FACING PAGE: *Augusta County's old Baylor Mill survived "the burning" campaign by the Union army in the Civil War, and it is a testament to the Shenandoah Valley's rich agricultural heritage.*

Just a couple of hours from the hustle and intrigue of the Capital Beltway lies an area of quiet and unpretentious beauty. Here, amidst the peaks, valleys, and foothills of the Blue Ridge Mountains, you can catch glorious sunsets, spot varied wildlife, walk in the footsteps of presidents, or simply find a peaceful escape along a mountain trail or winding country lane.

The Blue Ridge Mountains, which stretch from southern Pennsylvania southward into northern Georgia, are the easternmost ridge of the Appalachians. Formed 250 million to 300 million years ago, the Appalachian range is among the most ancient in the world. It is believed that at one time these mountains were as high as the Alps, but over millions of years, weathering has whittled them down to a mere snippet of their former lofty grandeur.

Still, with peaks protruding as high as 5,000 feet above sea level in Virginia, the Blue Ridge Mountains were formidable enough to keep the frontier to the west uninhabited by white settlers until the early 1700s, when German and Scotch-Irish farmers began moving into the area from Pennsylvania. These new residents settled into a wide, fertile valley that divides the Blue Ridge from the Allegheny Mountains to the west. They named this valley, as well as the long winding river that drains it, Shenandoah, from an Indian word meaning "clear-eyed daughter of the stars."

At this same time, wealthy English families from the Virginia Tidewater wanted to increase their land holdings and expanded westward into the foothills east of the Blue Ridge. These Virginia gentry established plantations and large country estates in the western Piedmont, where the gently rolling hills provided a perfect setting for their beloved foxhunting, an age-old aristocratic sport brought by their ancestors from Britain.

Throughout the region, small towns were established, initially to cater to the needs of the outlying farms, and they eventually grew into vibrant centers of commerce. The residents enjoyed years of prosperity until the ravages of the Civil War ripped a path of destruction across the land. When the war ended, families reunited and the rebuilding quickly began.

Today, much of the region looks as it did two centuries ago: farmland extends to the horizon; eighteenth-century taverns cater to travelers along old stagecoach routes; and Virginia gentry, mounted on magnificent thoroughbreds, chase foxes across rolling Piedmont pastures.

Along the routes in this chapter, you will encounter more than three centuries of American history—from the homes of four American presidents to the area's impressive collection of restored gristmills and stagecoach inns. Intimate involvement in the Civil War is evidenced by the profuse number of battlefields, monuments, and historical markers.

The area is also blessed with stunning natural attractions. You will discover trout-filled streams, tumbling waterfalls, ancient limestone caverns, and the grandeur of the mountains themselves. Whether you are exploring the lofty heights of their summits or enjoying the views of misty blue peaks from the roadways that wind through the foothills, the beauty of the Blue Ridge Mountains will never fail to inspire you.

Mossy Creek, which flows through Rockingham and Augusta Counties, is teeming with brown trout. It has been rated by Field & Stream *magazine* as one of the top five spring creeks in the nation.

RIGHT: *Oceans of corn line the roads near Springhill, in Augusta County.*

LEFT: *This bucolic scene of Mennonite farmland, complete with silos, barns, and grazing dairy cattle, can be seen from the Mole Hill in Rockingham County.*

ROUTE 1

This journey takes many twists and turns through Rockingham and Augusta Counties. From Dayton, take the following path: north on Virginia Secondary Route 701, left on Route 913, right on Route 736, left on Route 913, left on Route 732, right on Route 736, left on Route 737, right on Virginia Route 257 West, left on Route 744, left on Route 745, right on Route 752, left on Route 613, left again on Route 613, straight on Route 727, right on Route 747, left on Route 835, and right on Virginia Route 42 South. Bear right toward Mossy Creek Church where Route 42 makes a sharp left, then head straight on Route 747, left on Route 613/747, and left on Route 613. Cross Route 42 to stay on Route 613, and proceed through Springhill. Turn right on Route 742, right on Route 612, left on U.S. Highway 250 East, right on Route 612, right on Virginia Route 254 West, left on Route 708, right on Route 703/708, left on Route 708; note that 708 bears right at two Y intersections. Turn left on Route 876, left on Route 841, right on Route 711, left on Route 694, left on Route 700, right on Route 695, and left on Virginia Route 252 North to Staunton.

Virginia's Shenandoah Valley is a long stretch of lowland nestled between the Blue Ridge and Allegheny Mountains that features miles upon miles of unspoiled farmland. Grand views stretch to the majestic blue hills as you meander through Rockingham and Augusta Counties, Virginia's two largest agricultural counties. Here, you'll pass Mennonite farms, country churches, old mills, and grazing livestock.

Since the beginning of white settlement in the 1730s, the valley's prosperous farms yielded abundant crops and fattened livestock. During the Civil War, the Shenandoah Valley was dubbed "the breadbasket of the Confederacy" because it supplied much of the southern army's food supplies. As a result, in 1864, the Union army launched a campaign, known as "the burning," to destroy the valley's farms, crops, and mills and effectively cut off the Confederates' food supply. Many valley residents lost everything, but when the war finally ended, the resilient farmers returned to their homes and set out to rebuild what they had lost.

The little town of Dayton, one of the earliest settlements in Rockingham County, serves as your starting point for the tour. Daniel Harrison was the first to settle here, in 1745. His stone house, constructed in 1749, still stands as both a Virginia and National Registered Historic Landmark. During the mid-1700s, area residents used it as a refuge when they came under Indian attack, which earned the home the nickname Fort Harrison.

Dayton grew as a commercial hub for the Scotch-Irish and German families who settled in the surrounding farmland. Mennonite families began arriving in the 1780s, and today a thriving Mennonite community contributes enormously to the area's cultural and economic vitality.

Other points of interest in Dayton include the Shenandoah Valley Folk Art and Heritage Center, which features exhibits on valley history, and the Dayton Farmer's Market, an excellent indoor market with more than twenty shops that sell everything from homemade baked goods to folk art.

Just outside of town is the Silver Lake Mill, built in the early 1800s. In those days, the gristmill ran on the custom system, whereby the miller would grind the local farmers' corn and receive a portion of the ground product as his fee. The old mill was rebuilt after it was burned during the Civil War. It ceased operation in 1996 and is now the home of LDA Creations, a nationally renowned porcelain-decorating business.

After leaving Dayton, you will travel through the most scenic area in Rockingham County. Spring may be the loveliest season here: The rolling farm fields are mosaics of rich brown and intense green. There is an earthy aroma—a mingling of fresh air, tilled soil, grain, and natural fertilizer. At times, the latter can be a bit pungent.

In fenced pastures, alongside whitewashed barns and towering silos, black-and-white dairy cows graze patiently as they wait for milking time. Farmers on tractors plow the hillsides or chug slowly down the road as they travel between their fields.

Mennonites in horse-drawn buggies share the road. The clip-clop of hooves on pavement stirs up images of the nineteenth century. As the horses prance by, their antennae-like ears prick and turn, always alert to activities around them. Smiling faces peer out from the passing buggies and friendly waves are offered. Cute girls in bright cotton dresses and suspender-clad boys pedaling bicycles make their way to and from the small, country schools.

A particularly scenic spot on Virginia Secondary Route 913 has the interesting name of the Mole Hill. The "hill" is actually an igneous intrusion, approximately forty-seven million years old, that geologists believe is one of the last volcanoes that existed in present-day Virginia. The road climbs up and around the hill to offer a spectacular view of the farmland below. Tidy farms dominate the landscape, and silos form a rural skyline of sorts.

This historical photograph from the early twentieth century shows a farm family gathering hay with a horse-drawn binder. Courtesy Harrisonburg-Rockingham Historical Society, Dayton, VA

Only subtle differences are apparent as you leave Rockingham County and enter Augusta County. Beef cattle operations replace dairy farms, and the route passes through large, open tracts of pastureland. The views, both right and left, are magnificent.

Southwest of Staunton is another exceptionally picturesque section of the county. Although it has retained its unusually large agricultural tracts, the area is increasingly threatened by the land needs of a growing population.

As you circle Sugarloaf Mountain—a large hill that stands as a prominent local landmark—you will ramble through more bucolic farmland, past antebellum farmhouses, rustic barns, and grazing livestock. Baylor's Mill, located on Virginia Secondary Route 841, was one of the few mills left standing after the carnage of the Civil War. The mill, with its cut-limestone walls, was most likely built in the late 1700s by German Hessians who settled here after the Revolutionary War.

The tour terminates in Staunton, the "Queen City" of the Shenandoah Valley. With its wealth of elegant bed and breakfasts and excellent restaurants, this small, attractive city makes a perfect overnight stop.

Staunton's five historic districts are filled with gorgeously restored Victorian, Greek Revival, and Italianate architecture. Its charming downtown is packed with interesting shops and restaurants, historical sites like Woodrow Wilson's Birthplace, and the highly acclaimed Blackfriar's Playhouse, the world's only re-creation of William Shakespeare's original indoor theater.

The Frontier Culture Museum enlightens visitors by demonstrating the origins and lifestyles of the valley's early settlers. The museum includes a collection of working seventeenth- and eighteenth-century farmsteads that were transported to Staunton from Ireland, Germany, and England, as well as a nineteenth-century American homestead.

RIGHT: *At Staunton's Frontier Culture Museum, costumed interpreters demonstrate the Old World techniques for harvesting wheat.*

BELOW: *These horses are patiently biding their time in the "parking lot" of a Mennonite church near Dayton while their owners attend Sunday worship inside.*

Sunrise bathes an Augusta County farm following an overnight snowfall.

ROUTE 2

From Middletown, take U.S. Highway 11 South to Mauzy. For a side trip to Shenandoah Vineyards, head west from Edinburg on Virginia Secondary Route 675 (Stony Creek Road) and then turn right on Virginia Secondary Route 686 (South Ox Road). For Shenandoah Caverns, take Virginia Secondary Route 730 West just south of Mount Jackson.

U.S. Highway 11, through the Shenandoah Valley of Virginia, has a long and colorful history. Long before white settlers arrived in the area, Native Americans used the original buffalo path that preceded the road to move between their hunting grounds. In the 1730s, Scotch-Irish and German immigrants used the trail, which they referred to as the Indian Road, when they moved southward from Pennsylvania to settle in the valley. Eventually, it became known as the Great Wagon Road.

In 1834, the Valley Turnpike Company was authorized to build a sixty-eight-mile pike from Winchester to Harrisonburg. Soon after, another company built a similar pike from Harrisonburg to Staunton. The two companies and roads eventually merged into one ninety-three-mile turnpike, known as the Valley Pike. The road opened the Valley to travel and commerce—at a price. Travelers had to pay a toll every five miles.

The Pike was a key transportation link for both sides during the Civil War. During Thomas "Stonewall" Jackson's Valley Campaign, from March through June of 1862, he moved his troops and heavy artillery repeatedly up and down the Pike. He confiscated B&O Railroad engines and equipment from Martinsburg, West Virginia, and pulled them with horses down the Pike to Strasburg, where he sent them south on the rails of the Manassas Gap Railroad. One eyewitness reported seeing an engine drawn down the Pike by forty horses.

Union General Phil Sheridan also used the Pike during his Valley Campaign of August 1864 through March 1865, as he burned and plundered the valley from Winchester to Lexington. In reporting his destruction of barns, mills, and crops in a telegraph to General Ulysses S. Grant, he stated, "I have made the Shenandoah Valley of Virginia so bare that a crow flying over it would have to carry its knapsack."

The Valley Pike was eventually sold to the state and designated as U.S. Highway 11 in 1927. It remained the valley's major north-south thoroughfare until the construction of Interstate 81 in the 1960s. U.S. 11 still receives plenty of local traffic. For those not in a rush, it provides a relaxed and enjoyable travel experience. From nineteenth-century stagecoach inns to 1950s-era family-run motels and roadside diners, this route provides a glimpse of how life used to be—a nostalgic trip down memory lane.

This trip explores a forty-five-mile section of the Pike from Middletown south to the little community of Mauzy. The wealth of museums, battlefields, and landmarks associated with the Civil War will capture the attention of history buffs.

When the first settlers began arriving in the 1700s, settlements were established at roughly five-mile intervals along the Great Wagon Road. That distance was considered a town's service area, or the distance that residents could walk to shop or sell their products, and make it back home in one day. Consequently, the road passes through many small towns and villages. Each stop boasts its own historical significance and special character, as well as a wide variety of shops, eateries, and lodgings. Between towns, the land that is not designated historic battlefields remains mostly agricultural with farmhouses, barns, and grazing livestock dominating the scenery.

The trip begins in Middletown, the home of the Wayside Inn, an eighteenth-century hostelry and stagecoach stop that still offers valley travelers gracious lodging and fine food (like Colonial peanut soup!). The Cedar Creek Battlefield is the site of the last major battle of Sheridan's 1864 Valley Campaign. An annual re-enactment of this battle takes place on the weekend closest to the October 19th anniversary of the battle. The event draws up to five thousand re-enactors and ten thousand spectators.

The elegant limestone manor house at Belle Grove Plantation was built in 1797 by Major Isaac Hite and his wife, Nelly, who was the sister of James Madison. Courtesy Library of Congress, Prints & Photographs Division

Adjacent to the battlefield is the Belle Grove Plantation, an elegant limestone mansion completed in 1797 for Major Isaac Hite and his wife, Nelly, who was the sister of future President James Madison. The home and grounds are open seasonally for tours.

A few miles south of Middletown, the town of Strasburg sits at a strategic intersection that was a key location during both Jackson's and Sheridan's campaigns. Interesting exhibits can be viewed at the Stonewall Jackson Museum at Hupp's Hill and the Strasburg Museum. Known as the "Antiques Capital of Virginia," Strasburg is home to the famous Great Strasburg Emporium, where more than one hundred antique and art dealers sell their wares.

Woodstock was chartered in 1761 by an act of the House of Burgesses sponsored by George Washington. The town became the county seat of Shenandoah County. Thomas Jefferson designed its lovely limestone courthouse, which was built in 1795.

A restored nineteenth-century roller mill houses the visitors' center in Edinburg, a town that witnessed twelve skirmishes during the Civil War. The valley's oldest winery, Shenandoah Vineyards, is located a few miles from town. The winery provides an opportunity to taste a variety of award-winning wines.

Upon entering tiny Mount Jackson, you will pass a Confederate cemetery, another reminder of the area's Civil War heritage. The Old Union Church, which stands in the center of town, was used as one of the many field hospitals in Mount Jackson during the war; the walls inside the little brick church contain names, dates, and other messages scrawled by the wounded soldiers. South of town, just west of U.S. Highway 11 on Virginia Secondary Route 720, the Meems Bottom Bridge is Virginia's only covered bridge that is still in use. About a mile west of U.S. 11, Shenandoah Caverns is one of several public caverns in the valley; Shenandoah's lovely formations have been featured in *National Geographic.*

RIGHT: *Autumn leaves frame the bell tower of the old Union Church in Mount Jackson. The church, which was built in 1825, served as a field hospital during the Civil War.*

BELOW: *Vines, heavy with grapes, bask in the sun at the Shenandoah Valley's oldest winery, Shenandoah Vineyards.*

ABOVE: *The Battle of New Market re-enactment is held in May on the original 1864 battlefield; it is the oldest annual battle re-enactment in the nation.*

LEFT: *This old store is now a part of the Shoppes at Mauzy. It is reminiscent of the many general stores that once served the rural valley residents.*

New Market's quaint downtown has its share of antique and gift shops, but it is mainly recognized for its role in the Civil War. Most notable was the Battle of New Market: On May 15, 1864, 257 cadets from Lexington's Virginia Military Institute reinforced the dwindling Southern ranks on the battlefield and helped to achieve one of the last Confederate victories in the valley. The event is re-enacted each May at the New Market Battlefield State Historical Park.

The tour ends, as it began, at a former stagecoach inn. This preserved early nineteenth-century structure—along with a general store, a jailhouse, and a schoolhouse, also on the property—now holds a unique shopping experience known as The Shoppes at Mauzy. The shops are a treasure chest of assorted collectibles and gift items.

VIRGINIA'S CAVERNS

Virginia has nine show caves, or caverns, that are open to the public for touring. All are located in the mountainous area of the state, and most are in the Shenandoah Valley. The reason for this is simple: Caves form primarily in limestone, and the valley has plenty of limestone.

Acidic rainwater seeps through the soil to slowly dissolve and fracture the sedimentary limestone. The cracks widen, underground spaces grow, and the surrounding rock collapses. Over millions of years, this process creates underground systems with crystal-clear pools and beautiful geologic features such as stalagmites and stalactites.

The northern Shenandoah Valley is home to six show caves and each has its own notable features.

Crystal Caverns at Hupp's Hill in Strasburg was discovered in the 1750s and is considered to be the oldest documented caverns in Virginia. It is rumored that slaves hid here while seeking their escape to freedom. Crystal Caverns have the largest known concentration of calcite crystals in the Appalachian Region. "Frozen Falls," a crystallized waterfall, is one of the most celebrated formations.

Skyline Caverns in Front Royal is famous for its anthodites, or "Orchids of the Mineral Kingdom," that radiate in flower-like formations. "The Shrine" and "Capital Dome" are two of Skyline's notable formations.

Shenandoah Caverns in Quicksburg is the only cavern in Virginia with an elevator. The caverns have seventeen rooms, and the famous Bacon formations were featured in *National Geographic*. Other features include the "Grotto of the Gods," a large hall with drapery and calcite formations, and "Diamond Cascade," a huge calcite crystal formation.

Endless Caverns in New Market was discovered by two boys and their dog in 1879. No expedition has ever been able to find an end to the network of passageways. A wooly mammoth tooth was discovered here. Notable formations include "The Lodge Room" and "Fairy Land."

Luray Caverns in Luray is the largest cavern in the eastern United States and a designated Natural Landmark. It also has the world's largest musical instrument—the Stalacpipe Organ, an organ with pipes formed of stalactites. Other formations include "Titania's Veil," a pure white calcite formation, and "Saracen's Tent," one of the most perfectly formed drapery structures in the world.

Grand Caverns in Grottoes opened to the public in 1806 and is the nation's oldest show cave. It was ranked as the second-best show cave in America by *Parade* magazine, and it is known for its rare "shield" formations. Other notable formations include the "Rainbow Room," a large chamber lit with colored lights, and "Cathedral Hall," a giant room more than 280 feet long and 70 feet high.

ON THE CREST OF THE BLUE RIDGE

If you drive the posted thirty-five mile-per-hour speed limit and make no stops, it is possible to drive the entire length of Shenandoah National Park's Skyline Drive in about three hours. But, why on earth would you want to? Shenandoah is a place to escape from the rat race below. It is a place to slow down, unwind, and savor relaxing moments reconnecting with Mother Earth.

Begin your trip at the park's north entrance at Front Royal. Be sure to stop at Dickey Ridge Visitor Center to gather park guides and trail maps.

Skirting the crest of one of the most glorious sections of the Blue Ridge Mountains, Skyline Drive dips, climbs, and winds its way 105 miles south to its terminus at Rockfish Gap, where it intersects with the Blue Ridge Parkway. All along the drive, beautiful vistas unfold from overlooks that showcase the lovely Shenandoah Valley to the west. Many of these overlooks, such as The Point, provide the perfect vantage point from which to catch the spectacle of a Shenandoah sunset. Eastern-facing pullouts overlook Virginia's Piedmont and offer equally magnificent sunrises for early risers.

Archeological evidence suggests that humans have been present in these mountains for some eleven thousand years. For centuries, Native Americans used the land and hunted its wildlife. In the 1700s, European settlers arrived and began farming in the fertile Shenandoah Valley, at the western foot of the mountains.

As more settlers poured into the region, farmland became scarce. Farm families started to move into the mountains themselves, where they cleared the land for crops and grazing, and hunted the abundant wildlife. Later, large timber and mining companies commenced operations within these mountains. By the early 1900s, the once lushly forested mountain had been stripped of its trees and badly eroded. Its soil was depleted and unproductive; its wildlife was nearly eradicated.

As the National Park Service searched for a location for an eastern national park, local businessmen made a strong case for the Shenandoah region. In 1926, Congress authorized the establishment of Shenandoah National Park. The State of Virginia purchased nearly 280 square miles of land and donated it to the federal government.

Although many farmers had already moved out of the mountains because of depleted resources, the remaining residents were bought out or relocated, not all of them willingly. Crews from the Civilian Conservation Corps began work on what was to be a "novel experiment" to restore the overused lands to their natural state. Franklin D. Roosevelt dedicated the park in 1936 and the Skyline Drive was completed in 1939.

Slowly, the cultivated farmlands and stripped hillsides began to revegetate, first with shrubs and pines, then oaks, hickories, and other hardwoods. Today, mixed forests of evergreens and deciduous trees cover over ninety-five percent of the park.

The return of the mountain's forests brought the return of much of its wildlife. Today, more than fifty mammal species inhabit the park, including fox, bobcat, raccoon, black bear, and the ever-present white-tailed deer, as well as fifty-one reptile and amphibian species and two hundred resident and

ROUTE 3

From the North Entrance of Shenandoah National Park near Front Royal, take Skyline Drive south to the South Entrance of Shenandoah National Park near Waynesboro.

The skies above the Blue Ridge Mountains and the Piedmont beyond turn glorious shades of orange and pink in a classic Shenandoah sunrise.

ABOVE: *The gorgeous autumn foliage makes the Skyline Drive a favorite destination for leaf peepers.*

LEFT: *Upper Doyles River Falls in Shenandoah National Park can be reached by a moderate 2.7-mile hike. The park's many waterfalls are most magnificent in the spring.*

migratory bird species. These hills are alive with critters, and observant visitors are usually rewarded with frequent sightings. The highlight for families that make the trip in late spring and early summer is spotting the many white-tail fawns frolicking around Big Meadows or nursing from their patient, attentive mothers.

Though many people know the Skyline Drive as a prime trek for fall leaf peeping (the season usually peaks between October 10 and October 25), it is equally beautiful in spring and summer, with a riot of flowering flora. The green of spring climbs the mountains at a pace of about one hundred feet per day and reaches the highest peaks in May. Sweet-smelling pink azalea line the drive in late May, followed in June by prolific stands of mountain laurel with their dainty pink and white petals. Spring's bloodroots, trillium, and columbine give way to summer's Turk's-cap lilies, black-eyed Susans, and touch-me-nots. With more

GEORGE FREEMAN POLLOCK: FATHER OF SHENANDOAH NATIONAL PARK

On his first trip to Stony Man Mountain in Virginia's Blue Ridge, sixteen-year-old George Freeman Pollock was captivated by its rugged beauty. He immediately visualized creating a mountain resort there.

Eight years later, after acquiring the 5,371-acre Stony Man tract, Pollock organized his first camping party at Skyland (then called Stony Man Camp). In July 1894, fourteen guests made their way by foot or horseback up the rugged three-mile mountain trail to the camp, which consisted of several tents, a canvas bathing room, and a small dining hall.

From those humble beginnings, Skyland grew into an impressive resort that welcomed visitors with its gracious hospitality and magnificent scenery. The colorful Pollock, who was known for his unusual outfits, kept his guests entertained with Wild West shows and rattlesnake demonstrations. He frequently was seen riding through the camp on his horse, Prince, with his pet Pomeranian perched on the saddle. He also carried a bugle that he blew each morning in order to awaken his guests.

A lover of nature and the mountains, Pollock worked tirelessly over the years to preserve the area's beauty. He reportedly paid off lumbermen to leave tracts of giant hemlock trees standing, and he purchased other tracts outright, so that all of the magnificent virgin forests would not be destroyed.

The early 1900s brought talk of establishing a national park somewhere in the Appalachians. Pollock and other interested individuals worked diligently at persuading Congress to choose the area around Skyland for the site. As a result, Congress authorized Shenandoah National Park in 1926.

Located at the highest point on the Skyline Drive, Skyland today remains the heart of Shenandoah National Park. Many of the cabins and structures built in Pollock's days at Skyland remain for use by guests; they are preserved as an important part of the park's history.

George Pollock was well-known for his theatrics and flashy garb as the host at Skyland. Note the bugle, which he blew each morning to awaken his guests. Courtesy the National Park Service

than 862 wildflower species in the park, there is always something in bloom from March through October.

As scenic as Skyline Drive may be, Shenandoah is a park that should also be explored on foot. Don your hiking boots and get out of the car to fully appreciate what the park has to offer. Some 500 miles of trails—including 101 miles of the famous Appalachian Trail—lead to breathtaking views, spectacular waterfalls, and remnants of old farmsteads.

One of the best waterfall hikes is in Whiteoak Canyon. From the trailhead at Skyland, the trail descends into the canyon and follows along Whiteoak Run, passing by six waterfalls. The first, at eighty-six feet, is the highest and most spectacular waterfall.

A short hike on the Stony Man Nature Trail leads to the cliffs of the 4,010-foot Stony Man Summit. From a viewpoint on the cliffs, you are rewarded with a 180-degree view, which includes the Skyland resort below. Another favorite trail goes to Rapidan Camp, the former "Summer White House" of President Herbert Hoover and now a national historic landmark.

After pleasant days spent hiking, animal watching, and sunset gazing, you can retire for the evening to one of Shenandoah National Park's four campgrounds or two fine lodges.

THE PRESIDENTS' ROAD

As home to three of America's first five presidents, the drive from Sperryville to Charlottesville is a journey through the origins of our nation. With picturesque towns and parks nestled among the Blue Ridge foothills, it is also a scenic, beautiful region that is rich in opportunities for outdoor recreation. Local wineries and the historic sites of Charlottesville round out the varied activities to be enjoyed here.

Sperryville, a quirky little town at the foot of the Blue Ridge Mountains, is situated just below the Panorama entrance to Shenandoah National Park. Packed with antique stores, arts and crafts galleries, and specialty shops, this town is a joy for shoppers.

From Virginia Scenic Byway Route 231 (also called the Blue Ridge Turnpike), the rugged mountains form a constant panoramic backdrop as the roads wind through the rolling terrain. The route crosses and parallels rivers and trout streams, and it passes through tiny hamlets and miles of open farmland as it snakes along the foot of the mountains.

Grape-cluster highway signs point the way to a legion of nearby wineries. The first opportunity comes just two miles along Route 231, where a side trip right on Virginia Secondary Route 608 leads to the Smokehouse Winery. This unique Virginia winery specializes in historic beverages like meads, or honey-wines, called the Nectar of the Gods, and also entertains visitors with dulcimer performances.

For hikers, a side trip right off Route 231 on Secondary Route 601 brings you to the trailhead for Old Rag Mountain, one of Shenandoah National Park's premier hiking destinations. This strenuous eight-mile roundtrip hike

ROUTE 4

From Sperryville, take U.S. Highway 522 south toward Culpepper and turn right on Virginia Route 231 South. Just after crossing into Madison County, turn left on Secondary Route 602, then right on Route 603, and right onto Route 643. Cross Route 231 at Etlan and stay on Route 643 to a left turn on Route 600 and bear right into Syria. At Syria, turn left on Route 670, then right on Route 231 South to Madison. Leave Madison on Route 231 South. Turn left onto Virginia Route 20 North and proceed to James Madison's Montpelier. Leave Montpelier and head south on Route 20. Turn left on Route 678 and right on Route 777 to reach Barboursville Vineyards. Backtrack to Route 20 and head south through Charlottesville. South of Charlottesville, turn left on Virginia Route 53 to Monticello. Leave Monticello on Route 53 south and turn right on Route 795 to Ash Lawn-Highlands.

RIGHT: *Visitors to Shenandoah National Park are always thrilled to catch a glimpse of Ursus americanus,* the eastern black bear. *This young cub is one of about five hundred bears that live in the park.*

BELOW: *A whitetail deer watches over her fawn in Big Meadows, one of the best places in the park to watch deer.*

The delicate bloodroots are among the first of Shenandoah's wildflowers to bloom in the spring.

An ant crawls along the pinkish purple petals of wild geranium in Shenandoah National Park.

Shenandoah's colorful, late-spring palette includes the artful blossoms of columbine.

Mountain laurel is abundant in the rich, mountainous forests of Virginia.

(which includes a one-mile rock scramble to the peak) rewards hikers with magnificent views, prolific wildflowers, and possible wildlife sightings.

Turning left onto Secondary Route 602, the journey leads up to the crest of a hill where you can enjoy a beautiful expansive view of the weathered and craggy Old Rag. Be cautioned, however: This road crosses a low-water bridge that may not be passable during rainy spells without four-wheel drive.

Another hiking opportunity is available just west of the intersection of Virginia Secondary Routes 643 and 600. A side trip right on Route 600 leads to the trailhead for Shenandoah National Park's White Oak Canyon (also accessible within the park itself), a beautiful steep canyon with numerous grand waterfalls.

The main route of the journey turns left here and snakes along beside the Rose River—which later converges with the Robinson River, both good trout streams—and eventually returns to Route 231, where it veers away from the mountains into the Piedmont.

Just north of the town of Madison, a left turn on Route 638 leads to the lovely Hebron Lutheran Church. Built in 1740 by German settlers, the church is on the Virginia and National Registers of Historic Places.

The town of Madison, county seat of Madison County, was named for the Madison family, one of the area's largest landowners and the ancestors of President James Madison. The town holds a number of historic buildings, including the 1829 courthouse, and the Eagle House, which was originally a tavern when it was built in the late 1700s.

A left turn onto Virginia Route 20 will take you, in approximately three miles, to Montpelier, a National Trust Historic Site and the home of our fourth president and "Father of the Constitution," James Madison. This plantation was home to three generations of Madisons, from 1723 until 1844, when it was sold by the widowed Dolley Madison. Many additions and alterations to the original mansion were made over the years, including two large wings that were added during the Du Pont family's ownership in the early 1900s. A restoration is currently underway to return the mansion to the size, structure, and form of the President's era.

South of Montpelier in Barboursville, the Barboursville Vineyards and Ruins is an award-winning winery on land that was the former estate of James Barbour, governor of Virginia from 1812 to 1814. Barbour's good friend Thomas Jefferson designed the opulent mansion. The Barbour family occupied the mansion until it was destroyed in a fire on Christmas Day 1884. Reportedly, the fire started just as the family was preparing to eat their Christmas dinner. Undeterred, they carried the food-laden tables outside and continued their meal while the mansion burned. The stabilized ruins remain on the property and can be viewed by winery visitors.

Route 20 continues through beautiful rolling farmland with black-and-white board fences crisscrossing pastures filled with grazing cattle and horses. Large estates perch atop hillsides, all but hidden behind large, ancient trees. The terrain becomes increasingly hilly as the route heads back toward the Blue Ridge Mountains. Finally, it enters the city of Charlottesville, home to our third president and author of the Declaration of Independence, Thomas Jefferson.

At the southern end of town, a left turn from Route 20 onto Virginia Route 53 leads to three historical jewels. The first interesting stop is the Michie Tavern, an old stagecoach tavern that was built in 1784. The tavern was moved in 1927, seventeen miles away to its present location. In this rustic setting, hungry travelers can enjoy authentic Colonial fare—including fried chicken, black-eyed peas, stewed tomatoes, and cornbread—dished out by servers in period attire.

Jefferson's beloved home, Monticello—the name is Italian for "little mountain"—is located about two miles from Charlottesville on Route 53. A great lover of architecture, Jefferson designed, redesigned, and altered his Roman Neoclassic-style home over a forty-year period, beginning in 1769.

VIRGINIA: FIRST IN WINE

Wine making has been around in Virginia since the first English colonists arrived at Jamestown in 1607 and found grapes growing wild. The discovery sparked the colonists' hopes of wine making becoming one of their profit-making enterprises.

Their first batch of wine was made from what were most likely native scuppernong grapes, but it proved to be undrinkable. The colonists were not able to find a specialist who could produce a palatable wine from the offensive native fruit. The colonists even brought over a winemaker and vines from France, but the delicate French grapes could not tolerate the Virginia climate or pests. All efforts failed, even with the passage of Act Twelve by the House of Commons that required all male colonists to plant twelve grapevines.

More attempts were made over the years, but the efforts proved unsuccessful due to several factors: weather, pests, wars, and prohibition. Thomas Jefferson was a lover of wine, and he tried for thirty years to produce an acceptable wine at Monticello. He even requested the services of an Italian winemaker to help with grape experimentation.

A limited success was realized in the 1800s with the development of hybrid grapes, but it wasn't until an increasing nationwide wine consumption in the 1960s that Virginia farmers had a renewed interest in experimenting with grape growing. In 1976, an Italian winemaker sent his vineyard manager, Gabriele Rausse, to Barboursville Vineyards to grow European grapes. He was successful, and he helped other Virginia wineries by sharing his knowledge and grapes.

Since then, the wine industry in Virginia has exploded. From just six wineries in 1979, the Old Dominion now boasts more than a hundred wineries; the largest concentrations are in northern and central Virginia. It ranks fifth in the nation among vinifera grape-growing states, and the state produces a wide variety of award-winning wines.

More than 500,000 people visit Virginia's wineries each year, which is a major boost to state tourism. Roadside grape-cluster signs point the way to wineries that welcome visitors with tours, tastings, and a variety of festivals and other fun-filled events.

Adolph Russow (left) and two other principals of the Monticello Wine Company in Albemarle County enjoy the fruits of their labor in 1875. Courtesy Albemarle Charlottesville Historical Society, Charlottesville, VA

Barboursville Vineyards occupies the former estate of Virginia Governor James Barbour. The remains of the mansion, which burned in 1884, remain as a historic ruin.

Barboursville Vineyards, Virginia's most honored winery, is situated on 830 beautiful acres in the foothills of the Blue Ridge Mountains.

The West Front of Thomas Jefferson's Monticello, with its impressive dome and columned portico, is the classic view of the mansion.

Thomas Jefferson and his family enjoyed most of their meals here in the Tea Room at Monticello.

Thomas Jefferson's design for the Rotunda at the University of Virginia in Charlottesville was inspired by the Pantheon in Rome. It symbolized the enlightened human mind.

A visit to Monticello, including the house, stunning gardens, and plantation dependencies, provides an enlightening look into Jefferson's fascinating, multifaceted life and genius.

Your final stop is just a few miles down the road at Ash Lawn-Highland, home of the nation's fifth president, James Monroe. President Monroe, who was a good friend of his neighbor, Thomas Jefferson, owned the Highland plantation from 1793 to 1826. Later owners changed the name to Ash Lawn; today the estate is known by both names.

Although the trip formally ends here, you will probably want to include a stay in Charlottesville as part of your plans. There is a multitude of things to see and do in this vibrant city. Returning via Route 20 provides easy access to the Historic Court Square District, which is where British soldiers captured Daniel Boone while carrying out a raid on Charlottesville during the Revolutionary War. Also, plan to visit the University of Virginia. The beautiful "Grounds," designed as an "academical village" by the college's founder, Thomas Jefferson, is a World Heritage Site.

HUNT COUNTRY

ROUTE 5

From Aldie, take U.S. Highway 50 West and turn left on U.S. Highway 17 South to Sky Meadows State Park. From the park, take U.S. 17 North and turn left on Virginia Secondary Route 701 to Paris. From Paris, take U.S. 50 West to a right turn on Route 723 (Millwood Road) to Millwood. From Millwood, take Virginia Route 255 South, turn right on U.S. 50 West, then left into the State Arboretum of Virginia. In the arboretum, take the Loop Drive to Route 628. Turn left onto Route 628, then left on Route 626 to Long Branch Plantation. To return to U.S. 50 from the plantation, turn right on Route 626 and then left on Route 624.

Even though it is located just a stone's throw from the nation's capital, Virginia's Hunt Country could just as well be in a different universe, for all the similarities it shares with that pulsating metropolis.

U.S. Highway 50 rambles into the heart of Hunt Country, through pristine countryside and centuries-old villages filled with fieldstone houses and historic country inns. Old ivy-covered rock walls border magnificent estates where long, tree-lined driveways lead to elegant mansions, and pampered thoroughbreds loll about in fenced green pastures. The highway travels west, through Loudoun and Fauquier Counties in the Piedmont foothills, and then crosses the Blue Ridge Mountains at Ashby's Gap into the northeastern Shenandoah Valley.

Originally a Native American game trail, the path of U.S. 50 has been a major transportation corridor for centuries. In the seventeenth and eighteenth centuries, it was used by settlers moving westward from coastal Virginia and by traders traveling between the port of Alexandria and Winchester in the valley frontier. It was also one of the main routes used by Robert E. Lee and Stonewall Jackson during the Civil War. In 1982, the road was officially designated the John Singleton Mosby Memorial, after the legendary Civil War colonel. Mosby and his group of partisan rangers engaged in guerilla raids on Union troops in Northern Virginia.

Your journey begins in Aldie, an early nineteenth-century village filled with country inns and small shops. The town's beautifully restored Aldie Mill was built between 1807 and 1809. It is the only known mill in Virginia powered by twin overshot wheels (two wheels powered by water from above).

Next is Middleburg, known as the capital of Hunt Country, a designation that resonates throughout the town's multitude of shops and businesses that sport names like Hidden Horse Tavern, The Finicky Filly, and Cuppa Giddyup. Middleburg is where the owners and employees of all of those

grand horse farms come to shop, eat, and socialize. You will see everyone from jodhpur-donned billionaires in Mercedes SUVs to Wrangler-clad farmhands in mud-spattered Chevy pickups.

In 1728, Joseph Chinn opened an "ordinary" here, where travelers could stop at the halfway point between Alexandria and Winchester. A village grew up around Chinn's Crossroads, which was later appropriately renamed Middleburg. The town's Historic District is a designated Virginia Historic Landmark, and most of its original buildings are still in use today, including Mr. Chinn's ordinary, now known as the Red Fox Inn. The landmark structure has hosted notable clientele ranging from George Washington to Elizabeth Taylor and Jackie Kennedy Onassis.

The centerpiece of tiny Upperville is the beautiful Trinity Episcopal Church, which was a gift to the Meade Parish from philanthropists Paul and Rachel "Bunny" Mellon. Built in 1951 of local sandstone, the church is an adaptation of a twelfth- to thirteenth-century French country church. The entire town of Upperville is a Virginia Historic Landmark and listed in the National Register of Historic Places.

Middleburg, Upperville, and the surrounding countryside host numerous equestrian events, including horse shows, steeplechase races, and fox hunts. The Upperville Colt and Horse Show is an annual full-week event in June. Founded in 1853, it is the oldest horse show in the nation. The

In this historical photo from 1926, W. P. Hulbert of Middleburg is arriving with his guests for the annual cross-country race at the sixth annual Middleburg Hunt Cup. Courtesy Library of Congress, Prints & Photographs Division

The Aldie Mill is a magnificently restored 1807 gristmill with twin overshot wheels. Milling demonstrations are given twice daily on weekends.

The sport of foxhunting still reigns supreme throughout Loudoun and Fauquier Counties.

LEFT: *These handsome equines in Loudoun County are looking for attention from passersby.*

OPPOSITE PAGE: *In the village of Millwood, children play in the mill race of the Burwell-Morgan Mill. It is the oldest operable merchant mill in the Shenandoah Valley.*

Middleburg Spring Races, held annually in April, are the oldest steeplechase races in the state.

An ideal time to visit the area is during the annual Hunt Country Stable Tour, held every Memorial Day weekend, when many of the magnificent thoroughbred farms, such as the Mellons' Rokeby, open their gates to visitors. Other annual events include spring and fall farm tours, garden tours, antique and art shows, and wine festivals.

West of Upperville, Sky Meadows State Park is a beautiful 1,600-acre park that straddles Fauquier and Clarke Counties on land donated by Paul Mellon. Hiking and bridle trails reveal stunning vistas of rolling, green pastures dotted with barns and grazing cattle below. The park also provides access to the Appalachian Trail. In spring, the area is vibrantly green and in bloom with dogwood, redbud, and wildflowers.

You'll pass through the quaint village of Paris on your way back to historic U.S. 50, which now crosses the Blue Ridge Mountains at Ashby's Gap and enters Clarke County, in the Shenandoah Valley. After crossing the Shenandoah River, you will see more scenic horse farms on your way to Millwood. This sleepy little village was once a thriving commercial center that grew up around Nathaniel Burwell's merchant gristmill, established in 1782. The restored and operational mill, now the centerpiece of the village, is run by the Clarke County Historical Association as a mill museum.

Located a couple of miles north of town at the intersection of Routes 255 and 340 is The Old Chapel. Built in 1792, this historic chapel was the first Episcopal church west of the Blue Ridge Mountains.

Back on U.S. 50 West, the trip continues to the State Arboretum of Virginia, which is a part of the Blandy Experimental Farm and a University of Virginia research station. The arboretum's lovely grounds invite leisurely strolls through its various gardens and along the Native Plant Trail.

A loop drive winds through the farm, past a wetland, and makes its way to the entrance of Long Branch, an elegant Classical Revival mansion built around 1805 by Robert Carter Burwell. Mansion tours are available April through October, weekends only. The grounds of the 400-acre estate is the site of numerous annual events, including the Shenandoah Valley Hot Air Balloon and Wine Festival.

Although this drive can easily be managed in a day, the combination of pristine scenery, historical sites, quaint villages, fine restaurants and lodgings, antique stores, and superb local wineries may entice you to stay awhile to explore more of the backroads and varied attractions of Fauquier and Loudoun Counties.

John Singleton Mosby: The Gray Ghost of Loudoun County

Born near Charlottesville in 1833, John Singleton Mosby attended the University of Virginia. While there, he shot and wounded a fellow student with whom he had quarreled. Mosby was expelled, fined $1,000, and sent to jail for six months for his crime of "unlawful shooting." During his trial and imprisonment, he became interested in the law and acquired law books from his attorney. He was later admitted to the bar and practiced in Bristol, Virginia, until the start of the Civil War.

Mosby enlisted immediately and quickly rose to the rank of lieutenant. He distinguished himself while serving as a scout for Brigadier General Jeb Stuart. Later, seeking greater action and glory, Mosby sought to follow in the footsteps of Revolutionary War partisan hero Francis Marion, the legendary Swamp Fox. Under the Partisan Ranger Law, Mosby formed a group of men known as Mosby's Rangers and began guerilla raids on isolated Union posts and supply lines in Northern Virginia.

Mosby, along with his group of primarily volunteer Rangers, would appear in the night, seemingly out of nowhere, swiftly raid outposts, trains, wagons, and camps, and then disappear again without a trace. The tactics earned Mosby the nickname "The Gray Ghost." The Rangers would split up, hide out in area homes or the countryside surrounding Middleburg, and await the summons from Mosby for their next strike.

Mosby's fame grew with each successful raid. Union generals were frustrated by unsuccessful Federal attempts to stop him. An infuriated Ulysses Grant ordered all men under the age of fifty in Loudoun County to be arrested

Colonel John S. Mosby poses proudly in his Confederate uniform. Courtesy Library of Congress, Prints & Photographs Division

to keep them from joining the Rangers; he even considered taking family members of known Rangers hostage.

The flamboyant Mosby, dressed in his trademark red-lined cape and ostrich-plumed hat, continued his raids in this region, which was soon known as "Mosby's Confederacy," until the end of the war. By that time, he had earned the rank of colonel. He estimated that his operations had successfully kept at least thrity thousand Union soldiers away from the front line.

After the war, Mosby lived in Warrenton and resumed his law practice. He entered politics and even supported Grant's presidential campaign, which angered many of his southern friends. He served as U.S. Counsel in Hong Kong from 1878 to 1885 and as an assistant attorney for the U.S. Department of Justice from 1904 to 1910. He died in Washington, D.C., on May 30, 1916.

PART II

POTOMAC UPLANDS

ABOVE: *The Monocacy Aqueduct was often referred to as the "jewel of the C&O Canal." It was constructed from white and pink quartz sandstone quarried from nearby Sugarloaf Mountain.*

FACING PAGE: *Perched high on a hill in Harpers Ferry, the historic Hilltop House Hotel has a glorious view of the Potomac River. The hotel was built in 1888.*

The Potomac River is often referred to as the "Nation's River" because it travels through an area so rich in American history and heritage. The Potomac is also the common thread that binds this chapter together. Beginning in West Virginia, where the river itself begins, these trips travel through the Alleghenies, eastward to the river's fall line at Great Falls, and northwest of the Capital Beltway.

Originally called Patawomeke, the river's name has been shortened over the years. In the eighteenth century, it was known as the Patowmack, and finally it became Potomac. The name is derived from an Algonquian term that some say means "place where people trade." Given that it has served as a major route for trade and commerce since long before the first European settlers arrived, it is a logical and fitting name.

Most of this area was considered the frontier and remained sparsely populated until the 1800s, when both the railroad and the Chesapeake & Ohio Canal opened it to trade and travel. The earliest settlers here were plagued by hostile Indians before and during the French and Indian War of the mid-eighteenth century. Beginning with the 1859 siege of Harpers Ferry led by John Brown, the Potomac region saw numerous conflicts during the Civil War.

The geography and cultural makeup within the Potomac Basin differs considerably from the river's origin in West Virginia to the fall line. The river descends from the sparsely populated and rugged mountains of West Virginia, through the gently rolling farmlands of western Maryland, and on to the densely developed doorstep of Washington, D.C.

Consequently, the trips in this chapter access an incredible array of scenic and recreational attractions as well as historical sites that tell the stories, both inspirational and tragic, of our nation's early years. They offer you opportunities to immerse yourself in history, in a warm springs spa, or perhaps just to escape to the peace and tranquility of a mountain wilderness.

EXPLORING THE ALLEGHENIES

If you have a strong desire to get away from it all, this is the trip for you. This drive, into Wild and Wonderful West Virginia, takes you for a wilderness escape to the most scenic areas of the mountain state. Bring along your camera, hiking boots, and fishing poles, and be ready to explore.

The journey begins in Virginia, at Woodstock, from where you head west into the George Washington National Forest. Soon, you'll be climbing Great North Mountain, which is part of the Allegheny chain of the Appalachians. When you reach the top at Wolf Gap Recreation Area, you will be at the border of Virginia and West Virginia. An exhilarating, 4.4-mile roundtrip hike along the spine of Mill Mountain leads to a large sandstone outcropping called the Big Schloss. The name means palace or castle, and when you see it from the valley below (farther along the drive), you'll understand why early German settlers gave it this name. From the Schloss, incredible views reveal pristine national forest, distant ridges, and fertile valleys.

Back in the car, proceed down the mountain (now in West Virginia) into the lovely, agricultural Trout Run Valley. Near Perry, make sure to stop and

ROUTE 6

From Woodstock, follow Virginia Route 42 west and turn right on Virginia Secondary Route 675 (Wolf Gap Road) to Wolf Gap. Continue north on West Virginia County Road 23-10 (Trout Run Road) and turn left on County Road 16 (Mill Gap–Thorn Bottom Road) to Lost River. From Lost River, head south on West Virginia Route 259 toward Mathias. Turn right on County Road 12 to Lost River State Park. From the park, continue west on CR 12 and turn right on County Road 7 (South Fork Road) to Moorefield. Turn left on West Virginia Route 55, then left on U.S. Highway 220 South to Petersburg. From Petersburg, head west on West Virginia 28/55 to Seneca Rocks. For a side trip to Dolly Sods, turn right off of Route 28/55 onto County Road 28-7 (Jordon Run Road) near Hopeville, and then turn left on Forest Road 19 and right on Forest Road 75.

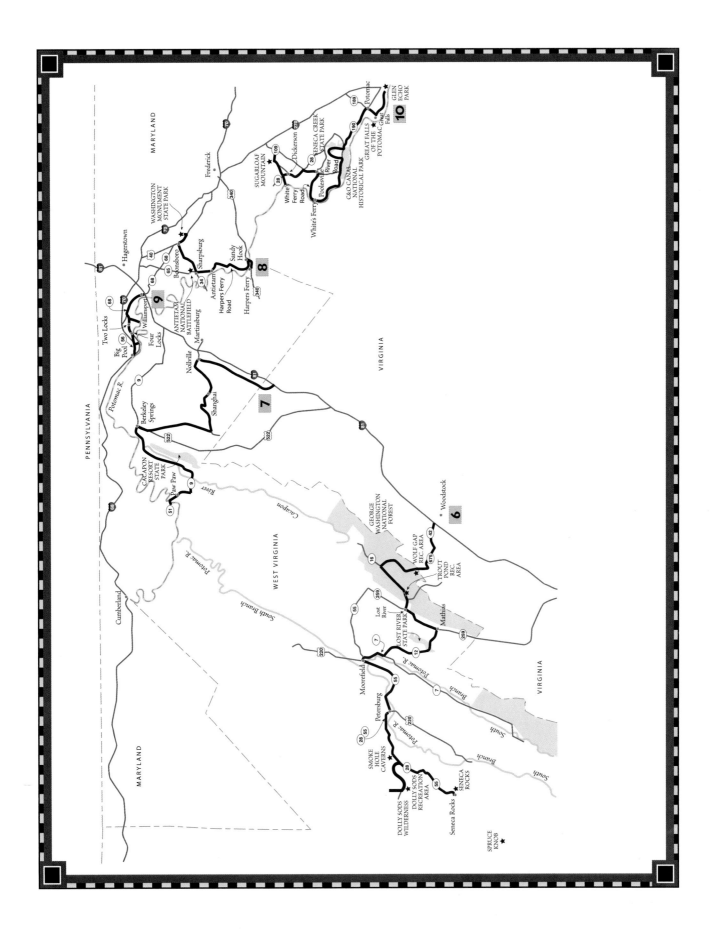

RIGHT: *This view from atop the Big Schloss on Mill Mountain in the George Washington National Forest overlooks the Trout Run Valley of West Virginia.*

OPPOSITE PAGE: *Seneca Rocks is a Mecca for rock climbers; the massive towers rise 900 feet above the valley floor.*

BELOW: *In autumn, the heath barrens of the Dolly Sods Wilderness Area turn a brilliant red.*

check out the view behind you to the east. You will see the Big Schloss protruding majestically from the mountaintop and looking very much like a castle.

The route now winds along the forested ridge to the Trout Pond Recreation Area, which is still part of the George Washington National Forest. The area is named for its trout pond, a one-acre water-filled sinkhole that is the only natural lake in West Virginia. The recreation area has a forested campground and picnic areas; hiking trails; and the seventeen-acre Rockcliff Lake for swimming, boating, and fishing. This is also a great place to spot wildlife; white-tailed deer are especially prolific.

On the way to Lost River State Park, you will pass through the small towns of Lost River and Lost City. The "lost" in all of these names refers to the Lost River, which is actually the Cacapon River. Just northeast of the town of Baker, Lost River disappears into an underground channel at an area known as "the sinks," and it reappears some three miles away as the Cacapon River.

Lost River State Park is a 3,700-acre wooded mountain paradise that is a perfect family retreat. The family of Revolutionary War general Henry "Light Horse Harry" Lee (father of General Robert E. Lee) owned a summer retreat here in the early 1800s. The cabin that Lee built is now a park museum. Park amenities include cabins, a swimming pool, tennis court, picnic shelters, and miles of hiking and horseback riding trails.

Next, the drive climbs over South Branch Mountain, along a winding road, and passes through historic Moorefield, the fourth-oldest city in the state. From there, it parallels the South Branch of the Potomac River and travels southwest through the broad farmland of the verdant South Branch Valley.

At Petersburg, you may want to stop for gas and supplies, because it is the last town of size that you will encounter for the remainder of the trip. From here, you head off into the wilds of the Monongahela National Forest, where finding supplies can be more challenging. The forest encompasses more than 919,000 acres of scenic mountain and forestlands in ten counties, and it includes the 4,861-foot-tall Spruce Knob, West Virginia's highest point. Situated within a day's drive of one-third of the nation's population, Monongahela National Forest has wilderness areas and outdoor recreational activities that are enjoyed by more than three million visitors each year.

After leaving Petersburg, you'll soon have an opportunity to explore West Virginia's underground at Smoke Hole Caverns. Home of the world's longest ribbon stalactite, these caverns also feature flowstone, columns, stalagmites, and even sideways-growing helectites.

Near Hopeville, a turnoff leads to the Dolly Sods Wilderness and Scenic Area, which makes a nice, but optional, side trip from the main route. The narrow, winding, dusty, bumpy, gravel road is slow going, but if you decide to venture on to see the "Sods," the reward is well worth the effort.

At Dolly Sods, you will find yourself in a windswept, tundra-like landscape that is more typical of Canada than West Virginia. It features low-growing vegetation, stunted trees, marshy muskegs, blueberry heaths, sphagnum bogs, rocky plains, and grassy balds or sods. The beautiful and mysterious Dolly Sods was named for the German Dahle family, who grazed sheep on the grassy sods in the mid-1800s. Its unusual landscape resulted from a number of natural and manmade factors. From the late 1800s through the early 1900s, loggers harvested Dolly Sods' magnificent red spruce forests and giant hemlocks. Then fires, accidentally or deliberately set, destroyed the exposed humus soil down to bare rock and created more open areas.

Dolly Sods' location—along the Allegheny Front on the eastern edge of the rugged Allegheny Plateau—and its high elevations—up to 4,000-plus feet—result in frigid temperatures and generous precipitation. Ice storms and heavy snows of up to 150 inches per year break the trees and shrubs, leaving them gnarled and twisted. Strong westerly winds cause the branches of flag-form red spruce trees to grow only on the eastern side, which leaves the western side of the trees bare. In spring and summer, stunted azaleas, mountain laurel, and rhododendron, along with myriad wildflowers, provide gorgeous color displays throughout Dolly Sods. In autumn, vast acres of blueberry fields turn a brilliant red.

While the Wilderness Area is crisscrossed by primitive trails suitable for experienced hikers only, the Scenic Area has trails for all skill levels, as well as scenic overlooks. The gigantic boulders at Bear Rocks are fun to climb, and they offer great vantage points for enjoying the fabulous views.

The drive continues through a forested valley, alongside the North Fork of the South Branch of the Potomac River, and soon arrives at Seneca Rocks, which is the terminus of the trip. Named after the Seneca Indian tribe that inhabited the area, Seneca Rocks is part of the 100,000-acre Spruce Knob-Seneca Rocks National Recreation Area. This magnificent formation of Tuscarora Sandstone was created some 400 million years ago when erosion stripped away the softer rock of the Allegheny Mountains and exposed the harder sandstone.

The cathedral-like formation rises nine hundred feet above the valley floor, and its sheer rock face beckons rock climbers from across the country. For those not into scaling rocks, there is a three-mile roundtrip hike that climbs the north edge of the rocks to a viewing platform. It is rather steep, but switchbacks, steps, and strategically placed benches make it doable for most anyone. The rewarding view down into the valley is breathtaking.

WARM SPRINGS AND TUNNELS

Orchards laden with sweet, juicy fruit may tempt you during the drive through West Virginia's eastern panhandle, an area of the Mountain State that holds an exhilarating variety of natural and man-made attractions. If picking your own fruit makes you a little stiff and sore, you might enjoy soaking in the same warm springs that George Washington frequented more than 250 years ago.

Beginning in the northwestern tip of Virginia, you will travel several miles through the orchard country of Frederick County, the apple capital of that state. Skirting along country lanes with whimsical names like Apple Pie Ridge Road, you'll pass acres of apple and peach orchards and lovely old farmhouses before crossing into West Virginia's Berkeley County.

ROUTE 7

From Interstate 81 Exit 321 at Clear Brook, head west on Virginia Secondary Route 672, then turn left on Route 661, right on Route 672, and right on Route 739 (Apple Pie Ridge Road). Entering West Virginia, the road is now County Road 26. Continue on CR 26, turn left on County Road 24, right on County Road 37, left on County Road 30, and right on County Road 15 in Nollville to Tuscarora Church. From the church, head west on CR 15 and turn right on County Road 18 to Shanghai; the road becomes County Road 7-13 west of Shanghai. Proceed straight through Shanghai on CR 7-13, and continue straight as the road becomes County Road 13-5. Turn right on County Road 8-5 to Stotlers Crossroads. Proceed straight through Stotlers Crossroads on County Road 13 to U.S. Highway 522. Head north on U.S. 522 and turn left on West Virginia Route 9 in Berkeley Springs. Follow Route 9 to Paw Paw. From Paw Paw, cross the Potomac on West Virginia Route 51 and turn right into C&O Canal National Park, at the Paw Paw Tunnel parking lot.

ABOVE: *Frederick County is the leading apple-producing county in Virginia and harvests more than three million bushels a year. In spring, the apple blossoms provide a feast for the eyes.*

RIGHT: *Ripe, luscious peaches are ready for picking at the George S. Orr & Sons Orchard near Arden, West Virginia.*

LEFT: *This small stone structure at Berkeley Springs is labeled George Washington's Bathtub. It is a reconstruction of the structures that were used by early bathers, including Washington, before 1784.*

BELOW: *Autumn shades of gold and crimson paint the banks of the Cacapon River.*

Bikers emerge from the darkness of the Paw Paw Tunnel, the largest manmade structure along the C&O Canal.

Soon after you enter West Virginia, look for the small log cabin of Colonel Morgan Morgan (yes, that really was his name), the first white settler in what is now West Virginia. Originally built between 1731 and 1734, the cabin was rebuilt in 1976 with many of the original logs.

The journey continues through bountiful farmland and orchards, which are particularly spectacular in spring when the orchards are in bloom. On the left, near Arden, is George S. Orr & Sons, a large farm and orchard operation. The farm's market offers pick-your-own seasonal fruits (or you can buy them already picked), including apples, peaches, cherries, plums, and strawberries.

At Nollville, a short diversion from the main road leads to the historic Tuscarora Presbyterian Church. Established by Scotch-Irish settlers in 1740, this is one of the oldest churches in West Virginia. Two log structures predated the present stone sanctuary, which was built in 1803. Ever mindful of the threat from hostile Indians, early worshipers brought their guns to church and hung them on wall pegs.

After visiting the church, you will twist and rollercoaster your way over three small mountains—North, Third Hill, and Sleepy Creek—while passing through tiny hamlets with names like Shanghai. You'll cross into Morgan County and then head north to the charming spa town of Berkeley Springs.

When the first Europeans found their way to this area around 1730, they learned about the medicinal powers of the warm springs from Indians who had been enjoying the magical waters for centuries.

In 1748, sixteen-year-old George Washington visited the springs while in the area with a survey party. In his March 18 diary entry, he wrote, "We this day called to see Ye Fam'd Warm Springs." After that first visit, he came regularly for many years to "take the waters," which greatly helped to promote the springs' reputation and fame as a health spa.

In 1776, Lord Fairfax, the owner of the land, conveyed his holdings to the Colony of Virginia. Soon thereafter, the land was offered for public sale. Numerous prominent Virginians purchased land here, including Washington. That same year, Virginia's General Assembly formed the town of Bath for the express purpose of caring for health seekers at the famous springs. The new town was named after the renowned English spa town and became this country's first spa.

Still officially named Bath, the town is now more commonly known by its post office name of Berkeley Springs. The 4.5-acre Berkeley Springs State Park (the smallest state park in the nation) occupies the center of town and surrounds the springs. The springs flow from five principle sources at two thousand gallons per minute and maintain a constant temperature of 74.3 degrees. Listed on the National Register of Historic Places, the park features an 1815 Roman bathhouse, a museum, a public drinking tap, a swimming pool, George Washington's "bathtub," and the main bathhouse, where a variety of spa treatments are offered. The town itself boasts five full-service spas, a country inn, fine restaurants, great shops and antique stores, and numerous galleries scattered around the downtown. Berkeley Springs has been named one of the "one hundred best small art towns in America."

West Virginia Route 9 out of Berkeley Springs is part of the Washington Heritage Trail, which links sites within the eastern panhandle that have connections to George Washington. Some three miles west of town, the Panorama Overlook at Prospect Peak offers a stunning view of three states and two rivers; it was rated by *National Geographic* as one of the five best views in the East. It was also one of George Washington's favorite horseback ride destinations when he was in the area.

From Berkeley Springs to the end of this trip, Route 9 takes a particularly scenic path. It snakes along the winding Cacapon River, and Cacapon Mountain rises alongside it to the east. Cacapon comes from a Shawnee word meaning "medicine waters." Cacapon Mountain, with a summit height of 2,300 feet, is the highest in the state's eastern panhandle.

The journey ends at Paw Paw, a tiny railroad and canal town tucked within one of the bends of the Potomac River. The name comes from the abundant paw paw fruit that grows wild in the area. It is the largest edible native North American fruit. It tastes like a cross between a banana and a cantaloupe.

Across the Potomac, in Maryland, is the Paw Paw Tunnel, part of the C&O Canal National Historical Park. At 3,118 feet long, 27 feet wide, and 24 feet high, the tunnel is the largest manmade structure along the canal. It was built to bypass a difficult stretch of the Potomac at the Paw Paw Bends, and its construction proved to be a long and costly ordeal. It took eight years to complete and was plagued with problems, including disease outbreaks, frequent cave-ins, and violent labor disputes.

These days, the tunnel is popular with hikers and bikers. The lengthy structure and its elevated wooden towpath make for a fascinating, though somewhat creepy, adventure. Make sure you bring a flashlight! At the halfway point, the openings at either end appear as tiny dots, and it's nearly pitch-black inside. Voices echo eerily off the walls and flickering flashlights cast spooky shadows. Needless to say, children (especially boys) love this place.

A ROAD OF WAR

Harpers Ferry, West Virginia, is a stunningly picturesque town tucked into the Blue Ridge Mountains at the confluence of the Potomac and Shenandoah Rivers. The scenic setting and bucolic character seem to belie the town's stormy and violent past, when it played a pivotal role in the nation's path to Civil War. An excursion to this region of West Virginia and Maryland is a journey through the history of that difficult time, but it also provides ample opportunity to explore more peaceful recreational pursuits.

The town of Harpers Ferry sits at the junction of three states: Virginia, West Virginia, and Maryland. It was named for Robert Harper, who started a ferry service across the Potomac and Shenandoah Rivers in 1747.

In October 1783, Thomas Jefferson described the beauty he saw from atop a rock outcropping, now known as Jefferson Rock, above Harpers Ferry: "The passage of the Potowmac through the Blue Ridge is perhaps one of the most stupendous scenes in Nature. . . . This scene is worth a voyage across the Atlantic."

ROUTE 8

From Harpers Ferry, take U.S. Highway 340 north. Turn right on Keep Tryst Road at the first exit after you cross the Potomac River Bridge into Maryland. Take a right on Sandy Hook Road and proceed to Sandy Hook and the C&O Canal National Historic Park. Head west on Harpers Ferry Road. (For a side trip to Kennedy Farm, turn right on Chestnut Grove Road.) Continue on Harpers Ferry Road to Sharpsburg. Turn left on Maryland Route 65 to Antietam National Battlefield. Return to Sharpsburg and head east on Maryland Route 34 to Boonsboro. Turn right on U.S. Highway Alt. 40, then left on Monument Road to Washington Monument State Park.

ABOVE: *A moderate four-mile hike leads to the cliffs of Maryland Heights and spectacular views of Harpers Ferry at the confluence of the Potomac and Shenandoah Rivers.*

OPPOSITE PAGE, TOP: *During the summer of 1859, John Brown rented the empty farmhouse of Dr. Robert F. Kennedy near Harpers Ferry. Here, Brown and his men prepared for their impending raid on the town.*

OPPOSITE PAGE, BOTTOM: *Washington Monument State Park near Boonsboro has the nation's first monument to George Washington.*

This Currier and Ives print from the late 1800s shows a view of Harpers Ferry from the Potomac River side. Courtesy Library of Congress, Prints & Photographs Division

While Jefferson looked at the convergence of the two mighty rivers as a beautiful spectacle of nature, President Washington viewed the same scene and saw an "inexhaustible supply of water" that could be used to power machinery. At his urging, a federal armory and arsenal were built at Harpers Ferry in 1799. Private industries, including sawmills, flour mills, and cotton mills soon followed. This growth, along with the arrival of the Chesapeake & Ohio (C&O) Canal and the Baltimore & Ohio (B&O) Railroad in the 1830s, turned Harpers Ferry from a wilderness village into a prosperous center of industry.

Yet, Harpers Ferry is most noted for the actions of famed abolitionist John Brown. On October 16, 1859, Brown and his twenty-one-man "army of liberation" attempted to seize the armory and arsenal as the first step in his plan to free the nation's slaves. Though his plot failed, it was one more step on the road to Civil War.

Harpers Ferry suffered tremendously during the war. Its location on the border between the north and south, the proximity of the strategic B&O Railroad, and the presence of the armory and arsenal, all made Harpers Ferry a hotly contested town. It changed hands eight times between 1861 and 1865. Factory buildings were burned, and the railroad bridge was blown up. When the war ended, the town and its economy were in shambles. Many residents had fled, and Harpers Ferry became little more than a ghost town.

Harpers Ferry never recovered as an industrial center. Due to its rich history, however, along with the area's natural beauty, the town began to enjoy a growing tourism business, which led to restoration efforts by the federal government.

Harpers Ferry was designated a national historical park in 1963. The park encompasses most of the nineteenth-century town, plus neighboring land in Virginia and Maryland. The town's complex history, which includes industry, transportation, civil war, and the African-American fight for freedom and equality, is all represented in the well-preserved buildings and museums within the park.

There are abundant recreational opportunities as well, including fishing, boating, and rafting. The famous Appalachian Trail runs through the center of town, and the trail's national headquarters is located here. On the Maryland side of the Potomac, the C&O Canal towpath provides another opportunity for hiking, biking, or jogging.

After leaving the area on Harpers Ferry Road, look for the turnoff to the Kennedy Farm. From late spring until autumn of 1859, John Brown rented this farmhouse from Robert F. Kennedy and used it as the staging area for his October 16th raid.

Back on Harpers Ferry Road, you'll drive through lush Maryland farmland, cross old stone bridges, and soon reach Sharpsburg, a quaint little village with lovely old stone houses. Antietam National Battlefield lies just north of the town.

Antietam marked the first of General Robert E. Lee's two attempts to take the Civil War into northern territory. During this battle, on September 17, 1862, more men were killed or wounded than on any other single day of this or any American war. The Union army lost a total of 12,410 men; the Confederates lost 10,700 soldiers. Although neither side could claim a decisive victory, the battle temporarily stopped Lee's invasion of the North. It also caused Great Britain to postpone its recognition of the Confederate government. Five days after the battle, Abraham Lincoln penned the Emancipation Proclamation to declare the freedom of slaves in all the states that were in rebellion against the Union. With this document, the purpose of the war became twofold: to preserve the Union and to end slavery.

Pick up a copy of the battlefield map at the visitors' center. An auto route takes you by the key sites of the battle, including the Burnside Bridge and Sunken Road (also called Bloody Lane). For nearly four hours, Union and Confederate troops contested this sunken country road; the skirmish resulted in more than five thousand reported casualties.

From Antietam, continue along the Shepherdstown Pike through the countryside of Washington County. You may wish to stop at the Crystal Grottoes Caverns, the only public show cave in Maryland. Opened to the public in 1922, it contains striking formations of delicate drape-like stalactites, bacon rinds, and columns.

A few miles past the town of Boonsboro, conclude your trip at the Washington Monument State Park, the site of the nation's first monument to George Washington. The citizens of Boonsboro dedicated the monument to the first president in 1827.

The rugged stone tower stands on the summit of South Mountain, a spur of the Blue Ridge chain. A climb to the top affords a wonderful view of the Cumberland Valley below. During the Civil War, the Union army used the strategic location as a signal station. These days, it's a great place for birdwatchers since the Cumberland Valley is a migratory bird flyway.

After the bloody Battle of Antietam, President Lincoln traveled to Antietam to discuss the course of the war. In this photo from October 3, 1862, Lincoln is meeting with Allan Pinkerton and Major General John A. McClernand. Courtesy Library of Congress, Prints & Photographs Division

On September 17, 1862, more than 5,000 casualties were suffered along this sunken road at Antietam, which became known as "Bloody Lane."

Burnside Bridge in Antietam National Battlefield was named for Union General Ambrose E. Burnside. The general's 12,000-man army fought its way across the bridge in an advance toward Sharpsburg.

A flock of geese pose in front of the C&O Canal's Conococheague Aqueduct in Williamsport.

Lockhouse 49 and remnants of the old locks can be viewed at Four Locks as part of the C&O Canal Historical Park.

John Brown was born May 9, 1800, in Torrington, Connecticut, to deeply religious parents who were strongly opposed to slavery.

As an adult, Brown entered into numerous business ventures, but none was successful. He struggled to support his large family, which consisted of twenty children from two separate marriages.

As his financial burdens mounted, he became increasingly philosophical. He incessantly brooded over the struggles and oppression of the nation's slaves. He gave land to runaway slaves, participated in the Underground Railroad, started an organization that protected escaped slaves, and even lived a short time in a black community in New York.

By the age of fifty, Brown was a militant abolitionist. He was obsessed with thoughts of slave uprisings, during which racists would be violently punished for their sins. He considered himself as the hand of God in carrying out that mission.

In 1855, he and five of his sons went to the Kansas Territory and worked to make it a haven for antislavery settlers. In 1856, after the free-state community of Lawrence was burned by proslavery vigilantes, Brown formed a militia that staged a revenge attack on a proslavery community. The militia dragged five unarmed men out of their homes and brutally hacked them to death with swords.

Soon Brown returned home and began planning in earnest for his war against slavery in the South. He formed an army of twenty-one men and rented a farm near Harpers Ferry, West Virginia, where he assembled arms and prepared for a raid on the federal arsenal and for the slave uprising to follow. On October 16, 1859, his army arrived in Harpers Ferry, seized the arsenal, and captured sixty prominent citizens in hopes that their slaves would join the fight—but none did.

The U.S. Marines, led by then-Colonel Robert E. Lee, arrived and quickly ended the insurrection. In all, ten of Brown's men were killed, five escaped, and seven, including Brown, were captured.

Brown was taken to Charlestown, Virginia (now West Virginia), where he was speedily tried and hung for treason. Before his death, he made an impassioned address that would resonate through the nation. His words inspired many to take up the cause of slave liberation and hastened the start of the Civil War.

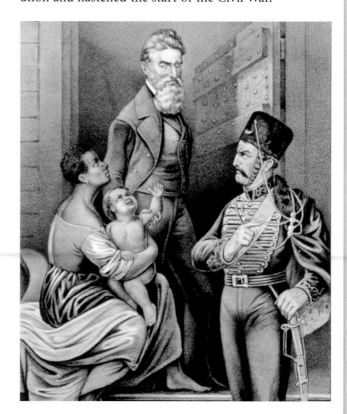

The Currier and Ives print entitled John Brown—The Martyr *shows a slave woman and her child meeting John Brown on the steps of the Charlestown jail as he is led to his execution.* Courtesy Library of Congress, Prints & Photographs Division

The tower has been rebuilt twice since 1827, most recently by the Civilian Conservation Corps in the 1930s. The park has picnic facilities, a playground, and hiking trails, including the Appalachian Trail, which passes at the base of the monument.

INTO THE FRONTIER

Washington County in northwestern Maryland lies within the scenic Cumberland Valley, which is part of the lush and fertile Great Valley that runs from Pennsylvania southward into western Virginia.

Created in 1776, Washington County was the first in America to be named after George Washington. In the early eighteenth century, this western portion of Maryland was the nation's western frontier, but English settlers were soon lured to the region by generous land offerings; German, Swiss, and Scotch-Irish immigrants eventually followed.

The English settlers did not fare well during the French and Indian War, which raged from 1754 to 1763. Many of them were killed and their homes and farms were burned by the French and their Indian allies. Soon after the war ended, a Michigan Ottawa chief named Pontiac encouraged tribes from the Ohio Country to unite with him in a massive uprising against English settlements in the northeast, including western Pennsylvania and Maryland. The settlers who had remained or returned to this area at the end of the war once again feared for their lives. Eventually, the rebellion was put down. With the safety of the settlers restored, the western expansion resumed.

By the mid-1800s, transportation and trade in this area were greatly boosted by the construction of railway lines and the Chesapeake & Ohio Canal, which paralleled the Potomac River from Georgetown to Cumberland, Maryland. Both of these transportation avenues were vitally important to the economic development of Washington County in the nineteenth and early twentieth centuries. Today, they serve as another type of economic draw: Both the canal and a retired section of the Western Maryland Railroad provide a wealth of recreational opportunities, from fishing and boating to hiking and biking.

Begin your tour of this historic county in the town of Williamsport. Located at the confluence of Conococheague Creek and the Potomac River, Williamsport was founded in 1787 by General Otho Holland Williams, a friend of George Washington. When Congress was searching for a site for the new nation's capital, Williamsport petitioned for consideration. President Washington inspected the town in 1791, but rejected it due to its off-the-beaten track location and its non-navigable waters.

Following the opening of the C&O Canal here in 1834, Williamsport became a booming waterfront town. When the canal closed in 1924 following a large flood, the town's boom days were over, and it reverted back to a sleepy little town on the Potomac.

Williamsport, considered to be an excellent example of a canal town, is the only place on the C&O Canal where so many examples of major canal structures can be found. A lock, a lockhouse, a re-watered section of canal, the

ROUTE 9

Begin at the C&O Canal National Historic Park Visitors Center in Williamsport. From Williamsport, take Maryland Route 68 to Maryland Route 56. Turn left (west) and proceed to Fort Frederick and the Western Maryland Rail Trail in Big Pool. To visit the canal, take left turns off Route 56 at Dam 5 Road, Four Locks Road, and McCoy's Ferry Road.

RIGHT: *Re-enactors at Fort Frederick State Park portray life during the French and Indian War.*

BELOW: *Articles from the French and Indian War era are displayed inside the barracks at Fort Frederick State Park.*

ABOVE: *The river plunges over a series of rocks and through narrow Mather Gorge at the spectacular Great Falls of the Potomac.*

LEFT: *A great blue heron tests his fishing skills in the tumultuous waters of the Potomac at Great Falls.*

Along the C&O Canal west of Williamsport, Dam No. 5 runs the width of the Potomac. Courtesy Library of Congress, Prints & Photographs Division

Cushwa turning basin, and the Conococheague Aqueduct can all be viewed along a half-mile stretch in Williamsport. A C&O Canal National Historical Park Visitors Center is located at Cushwa Basin in town.

Other interesting sections of the canal can be visited west of Williamsport, which are accessed by side roads off of Maryland Route 56. Dam No. 5 Road parallels the canal and river for about a mile and passes Dam No. 5, which runs the width of the Potomac River. A short distance from the dam is the ghost town of Two Locks, which served two locks that were located just one-tenth of a mile apart.

Farther along Route 56 at Four Locks, canal engineers designed a one-mile shortcut for the canal to avoid a four-mile loop that the Potomac makes around the neck. This design required the construction of four separate locks in order to accommodate the thirty-two-foot elevation change. Lockhouse 49 was built to house the workers or "lock tenders" who took care of the four locks and were available twenty-four hours a day to lock through the boats. As trade increased at Four Locks, other businesses such as general stores and feed stores opened up in the community. Today, you can see the remnants of the community, including the locks, Lockhouse 49, and a mule barn. There are also picnic facilities and a boat ramp available.

A short distance from Four Locks is the turnoff to McCoys Ferry, another access point to the Potomac. You will find picnic and camping facilities, a boat ramp, and a lovely view of the river. In 1861, this was the site of Maryland's first Civil War action: A group of Confederate soldiers attempted to seize the ferryboat that crossed the Potomac here.

Farther upriver is Fort Frederick State Park. Constructed in 1756, the fort was intended to protect the area's English settlers from attacks by the French and their Indian allies during the French and Indian War. While most other forts of this period were built from wood and earth, Fort Frederick was constructed soundly of stone. It was never attacked during that war, but it was used by the English as an important supply base. After the war, hundreds of settlers found protection within the sturdy walls of Fort Frederick during the uprising led by Chief Pontiac.

The fort was also used during the Revolutionary War as a prison for Hessian and British soldiers. The land was sold by the state of Maryland in 1791 and was used as private farmland for more than a hundred years. In 1922, the site was repurchased by the state and turned into Maryland's first state park.

The fort's stone wall and two barracks have been restored to their original 1750s appearance. Historical displays and historians in period attire help to interpret the fort's history. During the annual Grand Encampment in May, French, British, and Native American re-enactors from all over North America and Europe portray life during the French and Indian War.

THE CHESAPEAKE & OHIO CANAL

By the late 1700s, eastern merchants were anxious to find a navigable waterway that would connect the east with the rich resources of the Ohio Valley. Many, including George Washington, were convinced that the Potomac River, even with its perilous falls and rapids, was the most logical route.

Largely through the efforts of Washington, the Potowmack Company was organized in 1785. The company built five skirting canals that bypassed impassable sections of the Potomac and allowed small, raft-like boats to carry products to Georgetown. This system quickly became inadequate. Plans were soon devised to build a more reliable channel that would parallel the Potomac from Georgetown to Cumberland, Maryland, and on to the Ohio Valley.

The Chesapeake & Ohio Canal Company began construction on the canal on July 4, 1828, at Little Falls, Maryland. President John Quincy Adams turned the first shovel of dirt. The project was plagued by problems from the start. Labor shortages, disease, labor unrest, rough terrain, disputes with landowners, and legal battles with the B&O Railroad over the rights of way all slowed the progress. The cost of labor, materials, and land far exceeded original estimates. The engineering challenges of the project were enormous. The 185-mile canal included 74 lift locks, 11 multiarched aqueducts, and a 3,118-foot-long brick-lined tunnel. Consequently, long before the canal reached Cumberland, the company had abandoned its original plan of extending the system over the Alleghenies.

Sections of the canal were opened to traffic as they were completed; the first section opened in 1830. When the last section, Cumberland, opened in 1850, tonnage increased dramatically. Large quantities of coal were finally able to make their way east. In its peak year (1871), 850,000 tons of products traveled the canal with up to 500 boats operating at a time.

Many factors led to the demise of the Chesapeake & Ohio Canal, but the greatest contributor was railroad competition. An economic depression and three major floods added to the company's problems. By 1924, the railroad had taken over nearly all the commercial trade. Then, when another massive flood occurred, no repairs were made and the canal closed.

The federal government purchased the canal in 1938 and placed it under the control of the National Park Service. In 1971, Congress declared it a National Historical Park.

During its peak years, the C&O Canal could support five hundred boats at a time traveling between Georgetown and Cumberland, Maryland. Courtesy Library of Congress, Prints & Photographs Division

The park includes a riverfront campground and picnic facilities. The C&O Canal passes through the park, and the towpath offers hiking and biking opportunities. You can fish on the Potomac, which borders the park, and on Big Pool, a lake that was used as a two-mile section of the Canal.

The nearby town of Big Pool lies at the eastern end of the Western Maryland Rail Trail. This popular trail occupies about twenty-three miles of an abandoned segment of the Western Maryland Railroad line, from Big Pool west to Polly's Pond. It winds along the Potomac River, through woodland and scenic farmland, and passes many historical sites along the way. The trail's smooth, paved surface and gentle grade make it ideal for people of all ages and skill levels to enjoy hiking, jogging, or bicycling.

Children at Glen Echo Park enjoy a ride on the restored 1921 Dentzel-carved wooden carousel.

Park rangers in period attire at the C&O Canal Historical Park's Great Falls Tavern Visitor Center take visitors on a mule-pulled canal boat ride.

LEFT: *Cattails border a pond at the Homestead Farm near Poolesville.*

BELOW: *Picking berries at the Homestead Farm near Poolesville is a fun family outing.*

Route 10

From Glen Echo Park, head west on MacArthur Boulevard, then access Clara Barton Parkway, and proceed west. Turn left back onto MacArthur Boulevard and continue to the Great Falls area of C&O Canal National Historic Park. Backtrack to MacArthur Boulevard and turn left on Maryland Route 189 North, then left on Maryland Route 190 (River Road). At the intersection of Seneca Road and River Road, turn left to stay on River Road to Seneca. Turn left on Riley's Lock Road to visit the C&O Canal. Return to River Road and turn left, then right on Old River Road, and right on Montevideo Road. Take a right on Sugarland Road to visit Homestead Farm. From the farm, turn right on Sugarland Road. Turn left on Partnership Road and right on River Road. Bear right onto Mt. Nebo Road and continue straight at the intersection of Mt. Nebo Road and West Offutt Road. At Edwards Ferry Road, turn left for Edwards Ferry. From Edwards Ferry, turn left on River Road to White's Ferry. From White's Ferry, turn left on White's Ferry Road toward Poolesville. Turn left on Maryland Route 109, then left on Maryland Route 28. Turn right to stay on Route 28 through the town of Dickerson. Turn left at Mouth of Monocacy Road and proceed to the C&O Canal. Backtrack on Mouth of Monocacy Road, then turn left on Mt. Ephram Road to Sugarloaf Mountain. From the mountain, head west on Comus Road for Sugarloaf Mountain Winery.

Never more than an hour's drive from the Capital Beltway, a trip through Montgomery County in Maryland gets you out into the country. Much of this drive parallels the Potomac River and the Chesapeake & Ohio Canal, allowing you to make the most of this area's hiking, biking, and fishing opportunities.

The trek begins in Glen Echo at the Clara Barton National Historic Site, which is reached via the Clara Barton Parkway. Clara Barton was a humanitarian known as the "Angel of the Battlefield" for her work aiding wounded soldiers during the Civil War. She later founded the American Red Cross. The house, which she built in 1891, was her home for the last fifteen years of her life.

Across the parking lot from the Clara Barton house is Glen Echo Park. This former amusement park, which operated from 1911 until 1968, was acquired by the federal government in 1971. The National Park Service managed the park and collaborated with artists and organizations to create various art programs. The Park Service continues to manage the grounds, but the nonprofit Glen Echo Park Partnership for Arts and Culture oversees the facilities and programs. The park houses painters, potters, puppeteers, glassblowers, and other artists and performers. Renovations to the park's facilities have been ongoing and include its centerpiece, the beautifully restored 1921 Dentzel-carved wooden carousel.

The next major attraction on the route is the Great Falls area of the C&O Canal National Historical Park, where the canal shares the limelight with the Great Falls of the Potomac. As the Potomac River descends from the Piedmont Plateau, it builds up speed and force. At Great Falls, it plunges dramatically over a series of steep, jagged rocks and rushes through Mather Gorge to create a jaw-dropping spectacle. Beautiful to look at, yes, but the falls also created the greatest impediment to navigation on the Potomac. When the canal was constructed, the six-lock system that was devised to bypass the falls was a major feat of engineering.

Now serving as the park's visitors' center, Great Falls Tavern was originally built as the lockhouse, but it soon expanded into an inn. Here, you will find historical exhibits as well as C&O brochures, trail maps, and information on the mule-drawn canal boat rides. Several trails traverse the area, including the well-worn path to the Great Falls Overlook on Olmstead Island.

Upon exiting the park, you will pass upscale suburban developments on the way to the town of Potomac. Past Potomac, on River Road, the scenery becomes more rural as you approach Riley's Lock and the Seneca Creek Aqueduct. The old lockhouse and one of the remaining aqueducts, though not in very good shape, are both sites of interest. Nearby is Poole's Store. Built in 1901, this is the oldest general store in continuous operation in Montgomery County.

Montgomery County's Agricultural Reserve is a nationally acclaimed land-use plan that was established in 1980 to preserve the county's rapidly disappearing farmland. With nearly 600 farms and 350 horticultural enterprises, the reserve accounts for nearly one-third of the county's landmass. You will see fields of corn and soybeans, fenced pastures with grazing livestock, horse farms, and vistas dotted with barns and silos. At the Homestead Farm, a family-owned pick-your-own farm, you can pick seasonal fruits and vegetables, or browse through the farm market for jams, jellies, and pre-picked produce.

Another opportunity to explore part of the C&O Canal comes at Edwards Ferry, where you will find a lockhouse and the remains of Jarboe's Store, which was run by former lock-keepers. A ferry and bridge served this location, which was then known as Lock 25.

The next stretch of River Road is unpaved. As you travel along the gravel road, past acres and acres of corn and soybean fields, it will seem as though you are out in the middle of nowhere, when in fact, city life is just minutes away.

The Great Falls of the Potomac has long been considered a true spectacle of nature. Here, it is depicted in an engraving from 1802 by J. Cartwright of London. Courtesy Library of Congress, Prints & Photographs Division

The gravel road leads to White's Ferry, site of the last of the one hundred ferries that crossed the Potomac during the nineteenth century. Since 1828, a ferry here has transported travelers across the Potomac, to and from Leesburg, Virginia. These days, the cable-drawn, twenty-four-car vessel, named the *Jubal A. Early* (after a Confederate general) operates every day, from 5:00 a.m. to 11:00 p.m.

Leave White's Ferry on White's Ferry Road and travel toward Poolesville, which is a good place to stop if you need gas or food. If not, turn onto Maryland Route 109 just before you reach the town.

Historians describe the Monocacy Aqueduct, north of Poolesville, as one of the finest canal features in the United States. Completed in 1833, Monacacy is the largest of the C&O's eleven aqueducts. There are seven arches along its 438-foot length, each with a 54-foot span.

Next, the route travels to Sugarloaf Mountain, which is just over the county line in Frederick County. Sugarloaf, a conservation/recreation area, is privately owned and managed by Stronghold, a nonprofit corporation that was organized in 1946 by the late Gordon Strong. It runs the property for the public's "enjoyment and education in an appreciation of natural beauty."

Designated a Registered Natural Landmark for its beauty and geological interest, Sugarloaf Mountain is actually a monadnock, or a peak that remains after the surrounding land erodes. Sugarloaf's name came from early pioneers who said its shape reminded them of sugar. Back then, sugar was sold in loaves that were shaped into cylindrical mounds with rounded tops.

With an elevation of 1,282 feet above sea level, Sugarloaf has overlooks with stunning views of the surrounding farmland some 800 feet below. Here, you can enjoy picnicking, hiking, rock climbing, and horseback riding.

As a last stop, you may wish to sample the wines at Sugarloaf Mountain Vineyard, which is noted for its fine Bordeaux-style wines. The vineyard is located less than a mile from the mountain, on Comus Road.

PART III

FERTILE HILLS AND VALLEYS

ABOVE: *The sun sets over the battlefield at Gettysburg National Military Park.*

FACING PAGE: *A springtime drive through the orchard country of Adams County, Pennsylvania, finds hillsides covered in pink and white blossoms.*

efore the completion of the Capitol building in Washington, D.C., the center of the young nation's new government resided in Philadelphia from 1790 until 1800. Ever since its seventeenth-century origins as a colonial port, Philadelphia served as a magnet for immigrants seeking the promise of a better life in the New World, a life free of the religious and economic persecution that plagued their native countries.

From Philadelphia, German and Scotch-Irish immigrants migrated southwest along the Great Wagon Road to establish farms and homesteads in the fertile hills and valleys. From the early immigrants who settled just west of their port of entry, each successive wave pushed the frontier a little farther southwest, through the Blue Ridge region. It was not unusual for whole European communities to leave their ancestral homes and establish themselves, together, in this new and promising land. The Lancaster County region is an example of such a community.

The fertile lands soon rewarded them with crop-laden fields and orchards heavy with fruit. The immigrant communities settled into a new life of relative prosperity. But, sooner than they could have imagined, their new country was torn by conflict. Many had to watch their peaceful farmlands run red with the blood of fallen soldiers as countrymen fought one another in the American Civil War.

The grand agricultural vistas that early homesteaders brought forth are still evident in this region of southeastern Pennsylvania and northern Maryland. Quaint covered bridges, windmills, and barns made of stone and rough-hewn logs are leftovers from those early times, and today they dot the landscape among a patchwork of soil and crops. You will encounter natural areas that have been preserved as state and national parks, and journey to one region that experienced the carnage of the Civil War perhaps more than any other locality in the nation.

THE RESPITE OF PRESIDENTS

Northern Maryland's Frederick County features a veritable potpourri of attractions, including the state's tallest waterfall, the mountain retreat of United States presidents, a Holy Grotto, and two of Maryland's remaining covered bridges.

From the small town of Thurmont, the "Gateway to the Mountains," you'll travel west along the old Hagerstown-Westminster Turnpike toward Catoctin Mountain. This thirty-seven-mile-long mountain, which extends southward through Frederick County and into Virginia's Loudoun County, is an eastern prong of the Blue Ridge Mountains.

Various small Native American tribes hunted, fished, and farmed in the area long before Europeans began settling here in the early eighteenth century. The name "Catoctin" most likely came from the Kittocton tribe that lived at the foot of the mountain.

By the mid-1800s, the area along the nearby Monocacy River had been settled by German, Swiss, and Scotch-Irish immigrants, many of whom had

ROUTE 11

From Thurmont, follow Maryland Route 77 west to Cunningham Falls State Park. A left on Catoctin Hollow Road takes you into the park. From Route 77, take Park Central Road through Catoctin Mountain Park. Turn right on Buck Lantz Road, then right on Maryland Route 550. Turn left on Eylers Valley Road, and at the stop sign turn left to visit Eylers Valley Chapel. Turn right on Hampton Valley Road, right on Crystal Fountain Road, and right again on Annandale Road to the campus of Mount St. Mary's College. From campus, follow St. Anthony's Road and turn right on U.S. Highway 15 South. Turn left on Roddy Road and drive through the Roddy Road Covered Bridge. Turn left on Apples Church Road, then right on Graceham Road, left on Route 77. Turn right on Old Frederick Road and through the Loy's Station Covered Bridge.

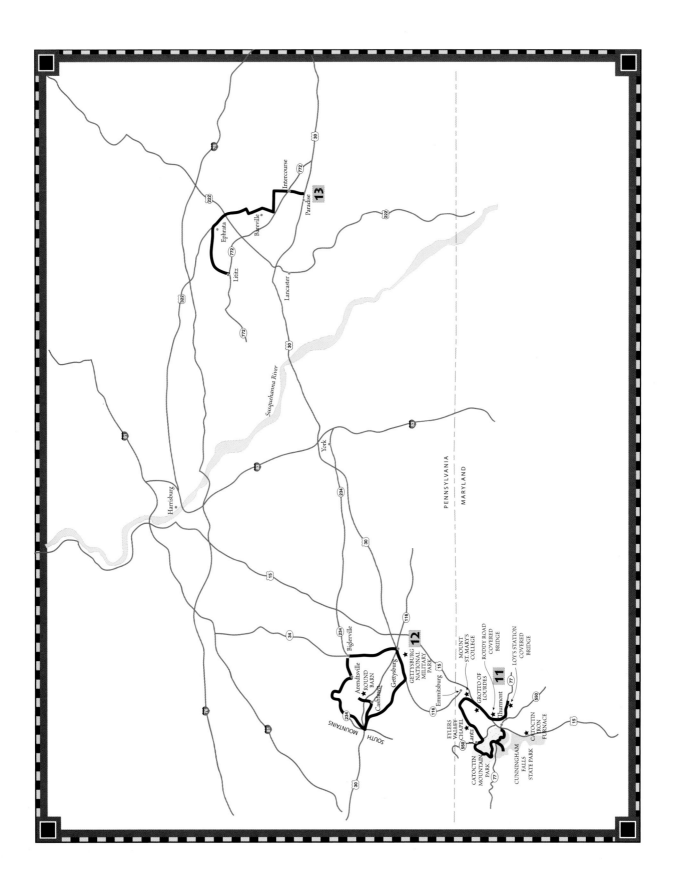

13

12

GETTYSBURG NATIONAL MILITARY PARK

11

Intercourse
Paradise
222
772
30
78
Ephrata
Bl'erville
Lititz
772
772
322
Lancaster
222

Susquehanna River

Harrisburg
81

York
83
83

PENNSYLVANIA
MARYLAND

234
30
15
34

Biglerville
234
116
Arendtsville
ROUND
BARN
Gettysburg
Cashtown
224

SOUTH MOUNTAINS

Emmitsburg
15
116
30
81
83

MOUNT
ST. MARY'S
COLLEGE
RODDY ROAD
COVERED
BRIDGE
LOY'S STATION
COVERED
BRIDGE
77
GROTTO OF
LOURDES
Thurmont
550
EYLERS
VALLEY
CHAPEL
550
Lantz
CATOCTIN
MOUNTAIN
PARK
77
CUNNINGHAM
FALLS
STATE PARK
CATOCTIN
IRON
FURNACE
15

The lovely little Eylers Valley Chapel has been serving worshippers since 1857.

LEFT: *An American flag is proudly displayed on this pretty farmhouse near Thurmont, Maryland.*

BELOW: *At seventy-eight feet, Cunningham Falls is Maryland's highest waterfall.*

initially settled in Pennsylvania before migrating here. Many began farming in the high valleys; others earned a living in the mountains logging, tanning, or working at the Catoctin Iron Furnace. These activities eventually depleted the mountain's natural resources and forced many residents to leave by the early 1900s.

As part of a 1930s Depression-era program that aimed to find new uses for marginally productive lands, 10,000 acres were acquired by the federal government. The land was developed as the Catoctin Recreational Demonstration Area with labor supplied by the Works Progress Administration (WPA) and Civilian Conservation Corps (CCC). Three camps were constructed for various uses within the development, including Camp Hi-Catoctin, which was built in 1938–1939 as a family camp for federal employees.

In 1942, President Franklin D. Roosevelt was seeking a location for a retreat to which he could escape the heat and humidity of Washington, D.C. The Secret Service, which was concerned about the president's safety during this time of war, found the development at Catoctin Mountain to be a suitable location. Hidden away in the coolness of the mountains and just sixty miles from the nation's capital, it was a safe and comfortable choice. The already constructed Camp Hi-Catoctin was converted into the new presidential retreat, which President Roosevelt renamed "Shangri-La."

After the war, President Harry Truman decided to keep the property as a presidential retreat, which would be maintained by the National Park Service. In 1952, he approved a plan to divide the property into two parks separated by Maryland Route 77. The southern half was designated as the Cunningham Falls State Park and put under the management of the Maryland State Forest and Park Service. The northern half, including the presidential camp, was named Catoctin Mountain Park and left under the control of the National Park Service.

After President Eisenhower took office in 1953, he renamed the retreat "Camp David" after his grandson. The camp still serves as the Presidential Retreat today, hidden within the park's boundaries and far from public roads and curious eyes.

Cunningham Falls State Park consists of two main developed areas. The Manor Area (accessed off of U.S. Highway 15) contains the remains of the Catoctin Iron Furnace, which operated from 1776 to 1903. This was once a booming industrial complex where a large group of specialized workers were assembled. There were houses for the workers, a charcoal house, casting house, foundry, forge, and sawmills. Much of this historical site is open for exploration.

The main recreational portion of the park is the William Houck Area, accessed from Route 77. Here, Hunting Creek Lake provides opportunities for swimming, fishing, and boating. Camping and picnic facilities are available in addition to a number of hiking trails to scenic areas, including Cunningham Falls. At seventy-eight feet, this cascade is Maryland's highest waterfall.

In Catoctin Mountain Park to the north, Park Central Road winds through the heart of the park and provides access to camping, picnic sites, and hiking trailheads. Wolf Rock, Chimney Rock, and Thurmont Vista trails all lead to interesting rock formations and views of the Frederick County countryside below. An easy trail, which leaves from the visitors' center, leads to the Blue Blazes Whiskey Still, where interpretive signs describe the moonshine-making stills that operated in these hills from the 1700s through the 1920s. The park also offers camping, trout fly-fishing, rock climbing, horseback riding, and wildlife watching.

Catoctin is delightful any time of the year. Spring brings the vibrant green of new growth and a prolific array of wildflowers. In summer, the lofty elevation provides a welcome reprieve from the lowland's sweltering heat. The mixed hardwood forest that covers ninety-five percent of the park ensures a kaleidoscope of color in the fall. During winter snows, the park's closed roads become paths for cross-country skiers.

After you explore these myriad offerings for outdoor activity, follow Park Central Road until it exits the park. You will descend through wooded foothills and high valleys and pass by lovely Eylers Valley Chapel (c. 1857) and Rainbow Lake. Soon, the buildings of Mount St. Mary's University and Seminary, the oldest independent Catholic college in America, come into view. Follow St. Anthony Road to the National Shrine Grotto of Lourdes. Upon entering the parking area, you are greeted by a golden statue of the Virgin Mary, atop the Pangborn Memorial Campanile. The statue stands high on a hillside overlooking the college campus and the town of Emmitsburg. It marks the former site of St. Mary's Church, which was built in 1805 by Father John DuBois, the founder of the university and seminary.

Enjoy a pleasant stroll through the beautiful grounds of the Grotto. This is the oldest replica in America of the grotto in Lourdes, France, that became famous in 1875 when apparitions of the Holy Mother appeared to a young girl named Bernadette. People of all religions are welcome at this peaceful sanctuary, where faithful pilgrims from all over the world come to pray and meditate.

The Grotto is closely linked to Saint Elizabeth Ann Seton, who lived in Emmitsburg from 1809 until her death in 1821. She was the founder of the American Sisters of Charity, which was the first native United States sisterhood, and in 1975, she became the first American-born canonized saint. Those interested in her life and work may enjoy a visit to the National Shrine of St. Elizabeth Ann Seton in nearby Emmitsburg.

From the Grotto, continue along U.S. 15, where lovely vistas unfold of farmland, orchards, and Catoctin Mountain. Look for the markets and orchard stores located along this route that sell an assortment of locally grown fruits and produce.

Turn onto Roddy Road and proceed one mile to the Roddy Road Covered Bridge. Built in 1856, this forty-five-foot, single-span Kingpost bridge still carries traffic over Owens Creek. Turning off Roddy Road onto Apples Church Road, you will pass the historic stone Apples Church. After several more turns, you'll find the Loy's Station Covered Bridge, another Frederick County covered bridge still in use. This Howe truss bridge, built around 1850, is the focal point of the adjoining Loy's Station county park, which is a perfect spot for a relaxing and nostalgic picnic lunch by the old red bridge.

ABOVE: *Built in 1856, the Roddy Road Covered Bridge is one of eight covered bridges that still survive in the state of Maryland.*

OPPOSITE PAGE: *Built in 1914, the Historic Round Barn near Arendtsville now serves as a farm market.*

ROUTE 12

Pick up tour maps at the Gettysburg National Military Park Museum and Visitors Center, and tour the battlefield. From West Confederate Avenue in Gettysburg National Military Park, turn right on Millerstown Road, which becomes Pumping Station Road. Turn right on Camp Gettysburg Road. Continue straight to cross Pennsylvania Route 116; the road becomes Knoxlyn Road. Turn left on Knoxlyn-Orrtanna Road, then right on Orrtanna Road. Turn left on Scott School Road, followed by a quick right onto Bingaman Road to Old Route 30. For a side trip to Cashtown, turn right (east) on Old Route 30. A side trip from Cashtown on Cashtown Road across U.S. Highway 30 leads to the Historic Round Barn. Proceeding west on Old Route 30 leads to U.S. 30. Cross U.S. 30, and within 100 yards turn right on Church Road. At the end of Church Road, turn right on Route 234. Follow Route 234 to a left turn on Excelsior Road. Turn left on Fairground Road, then right on Brysonia Road (SR 4008) to Route 234. Turn left on Route 234 and follow it to Biglerville. In Biglerville, turn right on Pennsylvania Route 34 and proceed to Gettysburg.

On June 30, 1863, the Confederate Army of Northern Virginia under the command of General Robert E. Lee and Union troops led by Major General George G. Meade met, by chance, at Gettysburg. The battle that ensued over the next three days pitted seventy-five thousand Confederates against ninety thousand Union troops. It was the bloodiest conflict of the Civil War. More men fell here than in any other battle ever fought on North American soil, with more than fifty-one thousand killed, wounded, or missing.

The three-day battle commenced on July 1 when Confederate forces attacked Union troops on McPherson Ridge, west of town. After managing to hold their position until after noon, the outnumbered Union forces were finally driven back to Cemetery Hill, south of town. Meade's forces were strengthened by the arrival of more troops during the night, and they gathered on Cemetery Ridge the next day. The Confederates were positioned on Seminary Ridge, a parallel ridge just one mile to the west. General Lee launched attacks on Meade's right and left flanks, but the assaults resulted in much bloodshed and little progress for the Confederates.

On July 3, more than twelve thousand Confederate soldiers advanced across the field toward the Union line along Cemetery Ridge in an attack known as Pickett's Charge. They were dealt a disastrous blow: More than five thousand casualties were inflicted in the span of one hour, ending the three-day battle. Defeated and exhausted, the Southern army retreated back across the Potomac to Virginia.

The Battle of Gettysburg came to be known as the "High Water Mark of the Confederacy," or the turning point of the war. Although the Civil War raged for two more years, the Confederate army never recovered from its enormous losses at Gettysburg.

For avid Civil War buffs, Gettysburg National Military Park is a Mecca. But even those with no real burning interest in the war will become quickly engrossed in the drama that unfolded on these hallowed grounds. You can read about it in books and watch it in movies, but nothing brings it home like standing in the very place where it happened. It is a deeply moving and emotional experience for most visitors.

Take advantage of the excellent exhibits and film at the Visitors Center and Cyclorama Center. Then pick up a copy of the National Park brochure, which includes a self-guided auto tour map of the battlefield. The eighteen-mile drive includes sixteen marked stops and follows the three-day battle in chronological order. Along the route, more than one thousand cannons and magnificent monuments mark strategic positions and honor the sacrifices made by those who fought here. The tour also makes a stop at the National Cemetery, the site where Abraham Lincoln delivered his famous Gettysburg Address on November 19, 1863.

As you drive through the battlefield—gazing out over the peaceful green fields, which once ran red with the blood of fallen soldiers—you will develop a new appreciation for the enormity of what took place here. If possible, visit

In this early photograph from Adams County, an entire family of pickers gets into the act at apple harvest time. Courtesy Adams County Historical Society, Gettysburg, Pennsylvania

the battlefield early in the morning, just before sunrise. At this time, there are few, if any, people; no cars; no noise. The predawn stillness provides the perfect setting to quietly ponder the tragedy of Gettysburg.

After your battlefield tour, a drive through the pastoral countryside of Adams County provides a nice contrast to Gettysburg's solemn atmosphere. This route closely follows the Adams County Scenic Valley Tour (a brochure for which is produced by the Gettysburg Convention and Visitors Bureau), and you will notice the road signs along the way.

Begin the tour by turning west on Millerstown Road from West Confederate Avenue inside Gettysburg park. You'll soon reach an entrance road for the Eisenhower National Historic Site, the home and farm of President and Mrs. Dwight D. Eisenhower. You may purchase tickets to tour the farm at the National Park Visitors Center, which runs a shuttle bus to the site.

Next you'll catch a view, to the left, of the 150-year-old Sachs Covered Bridge. To get a closer examination of the bridge, turn left onto Scott Road.

As you enter Pennsylvania farmland and the famous orchards of Adams County, you'll pass farmhouses, grazing livestock, and historic sites like the pretty stone Lower Marsh Creek Presbyterian Church, built in 1790. In the distance are the South Mountains, through which Robert E. Lee navigated his army en route to Gettysburg.

It will be obvious when you enter orchard country, as rolling hillsides lined with row after row of apple, peach, and pear trees come into view. This drive is spectacular in spring when the trees are covered with white and pink blossoms. Fall is equally appealing, when these same trees are heavy with ripened fruit. You'll find workers busily picking the bounty, and roadside stands provide the opportunity to buy some fruit to enjoy on your trip.

The words on the monument read:

> BATTERY
> E
> 1st. R.I.L.A.
> ARTILLERY
> BRIGADE
> 3rd. CORPS
> JULY 2.1863.

ABOVE: *Cannons flank Emmitsburg Road as it passes through the heart of the battlefield in Gettysburg National Military Park.*

OPPOSITE, TOP: *A statue of Brigadier General Gouverneur Warren looks out over Gettysburg Battlefield from atop Little Round Top, a strategic location at the southern end of the Union line.*

OPPOSITE, BOTTOM LEFT: *This statue of Mary Jemison stands in Adams County, near the site of her 1758 capture by four Frenchmen and six Shawnee Indians.*

OPPOSITE, BOTTOM RIGHT: *A monument at Hupp's Hill in Gettysburg National Military Park honors the 23d Pennsylvania Volunteers, also known as Birney's Zouaves, who hailed from Philadelphia.*

You travel next through Cashtown Pass and to the community of Cashtown. General Lee marched his army through this pass on the way to Gettysburg, and Confederate General A. P. Hill made his headquarters at the Cashtown Inn, while the twenty-two thousand men from his Third Corps made camp throughout the tiny town. The old inn (circa 1797) still stands and has been featured in numerous books and films, including *Gettysburg*. It offers bed and breakfast rooms and a fine restaurant.

The road climbs up to the summit of Mount Newman and passes by lovely St. Ignatius Loyola Church. Near this location, in the late 1750s, two white families were attacked and captured by four Frenchmen and six Shawnee Indians. All of them were later killed, except for a little boy and a young girl named Mary Jemison. Mary was adopted by the Shawnee and eventually married a Shawnee man. She became a very important and influential woman in her adoptive tribe. A statue of her stands near the church.

THE GETTYSBURG ADDRESS

On November 19, 1863, barely more than four months after the Battle of Gettysburg, a ceremony was held to dedicate the newly established Gettysburg National Cemetery. The cemetery was to be the proper, final burial ground for the thousands of Union dead who had been buried in shallow, hastily dug graves (if at all) following the battle.

The ceremony's principal speaker was Edward Everett, one of the nation's greatest orators. After delivering a two-hour oration, Everett was followed by President Abraham Lincoln, who had been asked to make "a few appropriate remarks." Lincoln then delivered the 272-word address that would become one of the most famous speeches in the history of the United States.

At the time, the speech received little attention. Many Lincoln supporters were disappointed that he did not use the opportunity to deliver a major address. However, the significance of the speech was immediately recognized by Edward Everett, who would later tell Lincoln, "I should be glad, if I could flatter myself that I came as near the central idea of the occasion in two hours, as you did in two minutes."

In his speech, Lincoln honored the sacrifice of the dead at Gettysburg, while reminding the living of the principles of liberty and equality that were established by our forefathers in the Declaration of Independence. He redefined the war as a struggle that would not only bring forth a "new birth of freedom," but would grant true equality to all citizens of the nation.

While it has been a popular belief that Lincoln hastily wrote his speech on the back of an envelope while en route to Gettysburg, he actually spent considerable time and thought choosing his words. He wrote the first draft while still in Washington and made revisions to it in Gettysburg, just before the ceremony.

Abraham Lincoln's now-legendary Gettysburg address was given at the dedication of the Gettysburg National Cemetery on November 19, 1863. Courtesy Library of Congress, Prints & Photographs Division

The summit of Piney Mountain affords excellent views of the valley and orchards below. From the summit, you will travel through a particularly scenic area known as the Narrows. The road winds through tall canopies of trees as it follows alongside Conewago Creek, a stream well known for its excellent trout fishing.

From here, you'll drive through more orchard country and the borough of Arendtsville before arriving in Biglerville. Known as "Apple Capital, USA," Biglerville is home to the National Apple Museum.

Following Pennsylvania Route 34 south from Biglerville takes you back into Gettysburg and the end of the tour.

THE DUTCH OF PENNSYLVANIA

Although most everyone is familiar with the area known as Pennsylvania Dutch Country, many are confused as to who the Pennsylvania Dutch really are.

The term "Dutch" leads many to believe that the original settlers of this area came from Holland. In actuality, the word came about as an English-language corruption of the word *Deutsch* (pronounced doitch), which is the German word for "German." In the eighteenth century, immigrants to this region of Pennsylvania came mainly from German-speaking areas of Europe, which included parts of present-day Poland, Switzerland, Czech Republic, France, and others, as well as Germany.

Also, many people equate Pennsylvania Dutch with the Amish. Although the Amish are Pennsylvania Dutch, not all Pennsylvania Dutch are Amish. During the 1700s, many German-speaking people immigrated to this area in search of religious freedom. These people included Mennonites, Brethren, Moravian, and other groups that fell under the broad category of Anabaptists, a religious movement in Europe that formed during the Reformation. The immigrants were mostly farmers in their home countries, and they found the fertile farmland of present-day Lancaster County an ideal place to settle.

An insatiable curiosity about the so-called plain people (Old Order Amish and Mennonites), who still maintain their simple, uncomplicated lifestyle, has turned this area into a major tourist destination. The main roads around Lancaster are crowded with motels, restaurants, and plenty of "plain people" attractions. Numerous shops sell beautifully handcrafted Amish furniture and stunning quilts. Farmers' markets offer homemade jellies, pickles, baked goods, and farm produce. And, of course, there are wonderful restaurants that serve up the rich and hearty Pennsylvania Dutch foods that guarantee a weekend weight gain of at least five pounds.

All that being said, the area's commercial attractions are not the main purpose of this trip. The route gets you off of the main roads and away from the hubbub so that you can experience the authentic and tranquil beauty of Lancaster County. You will follow a rather zigzagging route through the most scenic areas of the county, which explains the complexity of the route directions. Once you get into the heart of the farmland, the roads twist, turn, and

ROUTE 13

From Paradise, turn north off of U.S. Highway 30 onto Belmont Road and drive through Eshleman's Mill Covered Bridge. Turn right on West Pequea Lane, and turn left on Queen Road to Intercourse. Take Pennsylvania Route 772 (West Newport Road) north to a right on Centerville Road. Turn left on Scenic Road; a right turn on Groffdale Road followed by a quick left will keep you on Scenic Road. Turn right on Route 772, and stay on Route 772 as it bears right at the intersection with Harvest Road. Where Route 772 bears left, continue straight onto Hess Road. Turn left on East Eby Road followed by a quick right to stay on Hess Road. In Bareville, turn right on Pennsylvania Route 23, then left on Farmersville Road. Bear right, then left to follow Farmersville Road. Turn right on Schaeffer School Road, left on Saw Mill Road, and left on South Fairmount Road. South Fairmount Road becomes Cat's Back Road in Fairmount. Proceed on Cat's Back Road and pass through a covered bridge; the road changes to Cider Mill Road. Continue on Cider Mill Road and turn right on Willis Pierce Road, then left on Pleasant Valley Road. Turn left on U.S. Highway 322 and head west to Ephrata. Drive through Ephrata on U.S. 322 and turn left on Market Street. Turn right at the stop sign onto Rettew Mill Road, then a quick left onto Lincoln Road. Follow Lincoln Road to Brunnerville Road, and turn left to reach Lititz.

A group of Mennonite ladies tour the Ephrata Cloister, one of the nation's first religious communes.

An employee of the Sturgis Pretzel Company in Lititz demonstrates pretzel making in the original bakery's brick oven.

LEFT: *Interesting shops and boutiques invite browsing in charming downtown Lititz.*

BELOW: *An Amish youngster works the fields of his family's Lancaster County farm.*

This vintage postcard from the early 1900s shows Amish farmers at a curb market in Lancaster, Pennsylvania.
From the Voyageur Press Collection

at times seem to vanish due to missing road signs or roads that change names without warning.

Carry a Pennsylvania Gazetteer with you and don't worry about getting off course. You'll always find your way back, and a wrong turn will probably uncover something equally interesting.

Turning off of U.S. Highway 30 in Paradise, you'll drive through mostly Amish and Mennonite-owned farmland and soon pass through one of the county's famous covered bridges. The view spreads out before you in a seemingly never-ending tapestry of crop-laden fields, farmhouses, barns, silos, and windmills. You may feel like you've entered a time warp when you encounter the steady flow of horse-drawn buggies and observe farmers working their fields with teams of muscled, hard-working draft horses.

As you pass tidy farmhouses, with the day's laundry hanging out to dry in the breeze, it's hard not to wonder about the people who inhabit them. What would it be like to live without electricity, television, Internet, e-mail, or telephone? Hmm—it does have a certain appeal, doesn't it?

If you travel these roads on weekdays between 7:30 and 8:30 a.m. or around 3:30 p.m., you'll come across groups of Amish or Mennonite children on their way to and from school. Little boys with suspenders and broad-brimmed hats and little girls with cotton dresses and prayer bonnets on their pig-tailed heads make their way to or from their one-room schoolhouses. Some travel by scooter, their short legs pumping fast as they whisk down the roads.

In summer and autumn, roadside stands set up at the end of driveways offer fresh vegetables, jars of jams, pickles, and relishes, or homemade root beer for sale. Many operate on the honor system, with handwritten signs displaying the price and a box for the money.

Next, be sure to visit the Ephrata Cloister in the town of Ephrata. Started by Conrad Beissel in 1732, the cloister was one of America's first communes. Beissel was part of the reformist movement in Europe, until he was banished from Germany when his ideas conflicted with church laws. He made his way to Pennsylvania, where he affiliated with the German Baptists until his promotion of complete celibacy and Saturday worship proved too radical for them.

Beissel and his followers formed Ephrata, which was made up of celibate Brothers and Sisters who lived in separate quarters at the Cloister, and married couples, who lived on small farms just outside the Cloister. The members farmed and ran a publishing center, where they practiced the German art of calligraphy, known as *Frakturschriften*, or "broken lettering." They were also known for their beautiful self-composed a cappella music.

Leading an austere and rigid lifestyle, Ephrata members wore plain white, hooded cloaks. They slept in small chambers on hard, wood benches and used solid wooden blocks for pillows (ouch!).

Following Beissel's death in 1768, the society continued until about 1812. The remaining members formed the Seventh Day German Baptist Church, which survived until 1934. The Cloister's remaining twenty-eight acres and the log, stone, and half-timbered buildings were sold to the state and became a historic site in 1941. Tours of this National Historic Landmark and its lovely, park-like grounds are truly fascinating.

After exploring Ephrata, your trip ends in the village of Lititz. The village was founded in 1756 by the Moravians, another German-speaking religious group. This group, which claims to be the oldest Protestant church in the world, traces its roots back to 1457 when reformer John Hus led followers in the region of Bohemia and Moravia. All but eliminated during the Thirty Years' War, the movement was resurrected in the eighteenth century under the leadership of German Count Nicholas VonZinzendorf.

VonZinzendorf brought the church to Pennsylvania and gathered followers as he preached throughout the region. In 1744, some of those followers built their own church in Lititz, which they named after a town in Bohemia. Lititz was designed as a Moravian community, and only church members were allowed to live there until 1855.

The lively village is loaded with character, history, and charm. Its streets are lined with well-preserved eighteenth-century buildings and homes. The downtown is a shopper's delight with an eclectic array of shops and boutiques. The Lititz Moravian Church was built in 1787 and still graces the town's Moravian Square, as does Linden Hall, which was founded by Moravian Church members in 1746 and is the oldest girls' boarding school in the country.

In 1861, Julius Sturgis started Sturgis Pretzel Company here. It was the first commercial pretzel bakery in America. He baked his hand-twisted pretzels in the basement ovens of a house on East Main Street that was built in 1784. The business is still family-owned and -operated; tours of the original bakery, as well as lessons in pretzel twisting, are given daily.

Started in Philadelphia in 1884, Wilbur Chocolate Company moved its operations to Lititz in 1934. They're famous for their Wilbur Buds, which are tasty little chocolates that you can sample as you peruse the Candy Museum and Factory Outlet.

PART IV

ALONG THE DELAWARE

ABOVE: *Low-flying snow geese pass over Bombay Hook National Wildlife Refuge at sunrise.*

FACING PAGE: *The Sheriff's home and an arsenal in the distance stand along The Green in the center of historic New Castle.*

In the early seventeenth century, small groups of intrepid European colonists entered the Delaware Bay, sailed up the Delaware River, and established settlements in present-day Delaware. The Dutch were the first to arrive, in 1631, followed by Swedish, Finnish, and English settlers. Subsequently, this region was fought over, claimed, and reclaimed by these different groups until the English took permanent control in 1674.

In 1682, Delaware was included in the land grant from England's King Charles that gave William Penn all of Pennsylvania. Among the new arrivals who first settled in the Wilmington area were members of the Society of Friends, better known as Quakers. Joining other early settlers who had already migrated northward from Wilmington, the Quakers established meeting-houses, mills, and farms in the lush and beautiful Brandywine River Valley. This valley would later become the center of the Du Pont family empire.

Further exploration of Delaware's coast will take you to small towns and villages along the Delaware River and the Delaware Bay that hold a wealth of historic attractions. Beautifully preserved colonial architecture, Chesapeake & Delaware Canal history, and former military forts all offer opportunities to learn about coastal Delaware's past.

Due to its location along the Atlantic Flyway, coastal Delaware is teeming with wildlife. All along the way, there are numerous parks and wildlife refuges from which to observe it.

You will also visit historic Lewes, which was the site of the first settlement in present-day Delaware. Then sail across the Delaware Bay via ferry to explore Cape May, New Jersey, a picturesque Victorian town known as "America's first and oldest seashore resort."

IN THE VALLEY OF THE BRANDYWINE

ROUTE 14

From Brandywine Battlefield State Park, take U.S. Highway 1 South to Route 100. (It is Route 100 in both Pennsylvania and Delaware.) Turn left on Route 100 and follow it to Delaware Route 141. Turn left (east) on Route 141 to reach The Hagley Museum. From the museum, backtrack on Route 141 and proceed to Route 52. Turn right on Route 52 and follow it north to U.S. 1. Turn left on U.S. 1 South to Longwood Gardens.

The Brandywine Valley stretches from northern Delaware into southeastern Pennsylvania. Carved out by the Brandywine River, this picturesque valley has managed to retain much of its rural flavor, even though it is located just minutes from the Wilmington and Philadelphia urban centers. As you travel along the winding country roads past rambling estates and horse farms, you may forget that towering city skylines loom just over the hill.

The first European settlers in the Brandywine Valley were Swedish and Finnish soldiers and adventurers. In 1638, they established a fort and trading post in present-day Wilmington and eventually moved farther upriver into the valley. The first English settlers, including many Quakers, moved into the valley in the 1680s. They established large farms and built mills along the creeks of the Brandywine.

During the American Revolution, the valley's proximity to the Colonial capital of Philadelphia made it a key front in the war. Your journey begins at Brandywine Battlefield State Park in Pennsylvania. In September 1777, fifteen thousand British and Hessian soldiers, led by General William Howe, were advancing toward Philadelphia. George Washington's eleven thousand Continentals met them at Chadds Ford, about thirty miles from the Colonial

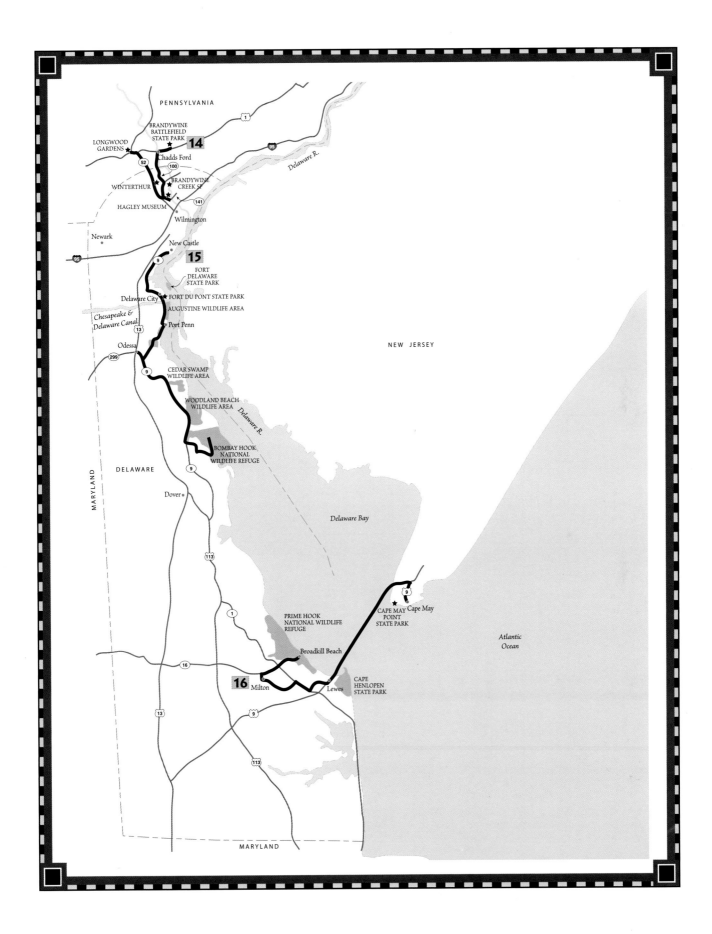

PENNSYLVANIA

BRANDYWINE
BATTLEFIELD
STATE PARK

14

LONGWOOD
GARDENS

①

Chadds Ford

⑩

WINTERTHUR

BRANDYWINE
CREEK SP

HAGLEY MUSEUM

⑭⑪

Delaware R.

Wilmington

Newark

New Castle

⑨

15

FORT
DELAWARE
STATE PARK

Delaware City ★ FORT DU PONT STATE PARK

AUGUSTINE WILDLIFE AREA

Chesapeake &
Delaware Canal

⑬ Port Penn

Odessa

㉙⑨

CEDAR SWAMP
WILDLIFE AREA

WOODLAND BEACH
WILDLIFE AREA

Delaware R.

NEW JERSEY

⑨

BOMBAY HOOK
NATIONAL
WILDLIFE REFUGE

MARYLAND

DELAWARE

Dover

⑪⑬

Delaware Bay

①

PRIME HOOK
NATIONAL
WILDLIFE
REFUGE

CAPE MAY Cape May
POINT
STATE PARK

⑨

Atlantic
Ocean

Broadkill Beach

⑯

16 Milton

⑬

⑨

⑪⑬

CAPE
HENLOPEN
STATE PARK

Lewes

MARYLAND

OPPOSITE PAGE: *Flowering dogwood trees add a touch of spring color to the Powder Yard at the Hagley Museum near Wilmington.*

RIGHT: *When planning his gardens at the Winterthur estate, Henry Francis du Pont chose combinations of plantings that would ensure a continuous bloom from late January through November.*

BELOW: *The Marquis de Lafayette was just nineteen years old when he saw his first military action in America at the Battle of the Brandywine. He was quartered at this house, the home of Quaker farmer Gideon Gilpin.*

capital, and attempted to stop their advance. On September 11, the two sides clashed at the Battle of the Brandywine, which was the largest land battle of the war. The British won the hard-fought battle and seized Philadelphia on September 26.

The historic battlefield is preserved in a fifty-acre park that contains a museum with displays of weapons, uniforms, and other artifacts and exhibits. Also within the park is the house that served as Washington's headquarters, and the home where nineteen-year-old Marquis de Lafayette was quartered.

Just two miles from the battlefield, the Brandywine River Museum occupies a converted nineteenth-century gristmill on the banks of the river. Often called the "Wyeth Museum" because of its extensive collection of works by three generations of the Wyeth family (N. C., Andrew, and Jamie), it also exhibits the works of many other artists and illustrators. Outside, the Wildflower and Native Plant Gardens add a splash of brilliant color to a cobblestone courtyard and paths leading to the river.

Over the last two centuries, the greatest influence on the Brandywine Valley has been the Du Pont family. Since the family's arrival in 1802, the businesses, wealth, and philanthropy of the Du Ponts have had a huge impact on the area's landscape as well as its economy. Throughout the valley are parklands, opulent mansions, and glorious gardens that were bequeathed to the public by the Du Ponts.

Delaware's Brandywine Creek State Park is a 933-acre former Du Pont family dairy farm. This lovely park has open grassy fields dotted with wildflowers and divided by gray stone walls that were built from local stone in the 1800s. Two nature preserves and fourteen miles of trails are perfect for spotting wildlife.

At the Hagley Museum and Library/Eleutherian Mills just outside of Wilmington, you will see where the Du Pont family dynasty began in America. Eleuthère Irénée du Pont (better known as E. I.) fled to America from France in 1799, during the French Revolution. In 1802, he acquired land on the Brandywine River and began building black-powder mills. He would soon become the largest American manufacturer of the explosive.

The site's history is documented in a collection of exhibits and dioramas in the visitors' center. In the old powder yard, several original buildings and structures—including rolling mills, millwright shop, and machine shops—house exhibits and machinery. Interpreters demonstrate various facets of the powder-making process. All of this is located in an extremely picturesque setting along the river. Flowering dogwoods, redbuds, and azaleas make it particularly inviting in the spring.

The first home of E. I. du Pont sits on a hill above the powder yard. Built in 1803, the lovely Georgian-style house is furnished with antiques and Du Pont memorabilia. E. I., an avid botanist, designed the French-style garden adjacent to the house.

Next along the drive is Winterthur Museum & Country Estate. It was purchased in 1837 by E. I. du Pont's daughter, Evelina, and her husband, James Biderman. The home was named after Biderman's ancestral home in Switzerland. Winterthur became the property of Henry Francis du Pont, the great-grandson of E. I. du Pont, in 1927. In 1951, it was opened to the public under management of the Winterthur Corporation, a nonprofit educational foundation.

The mansion houses the museum, which consists of 175 period rooms filled with the extensive collection of furniture and early American decorative arts acquired by Henry Francis du Pont. An additional wing built in 1992 contains three exhibition galleries. The estate sits on 982 acres that include 60 acres of naturalistic garden. Du Pont chose plants from around the world to fit into his landscaping plan and to create harmonious color combinations.

Crossing back into Pennsylvania, your final stop on this drive is Longwood Gardens, a horticultural extravaganza created by E. I. du Pont's great grandson, Pierre S. du Pont.

A Quaker family by the name of Pierce purchased the Longwood property from William Penn in 1700 and established a farm. In 1798, the family planted an arboretum, and by 1850, it had become one of the finest tree collections in the country.

Pierre du Pont purchased the property in 1906, intent on preserving its tree collection. An interest in horticulture and gardening ran in the Du Pont family, and with the creation of Longwood Gardens, Pierre proved to be the family's gardener extraordinaire.

From 1907 to the late 1930s, Pierre created most of what you see at Longwood today. Following no grand overall plan, he created the gardens one by one. He was influenced by a variety of gardens, ideas, and technologies that he had encountered during his extensive world travels.

In 1937, Pierre founded the Longwood Foundation to handle his philanthropic activities, and in 1946, the gardens were turned over to the foundation "for the sole use of the public for purposes of exhibition, instruction, education, and enjoyment."

You could easily spend an entire day at Longwood. The property includes the manor house; 1,050 acres of gardens, woodlands, and meadows; a twenty-room conservatory; and more fountains than any other garden in the world. One of the most popular exhibits is the Orchid House, which contains 3,200 different orchid varieties, with 200 to 500 orchids at peak bloom at any given time.

The Du Pont powder mill on the Brandywine River operated for 118 years, from 1803 until 1921. Courtesy Library of Congress, Prints & Photographs Division

COLONIAL FLYWAY

Historic Delaware River port towns and beautiful marshlands teeming with wildlife await you on this drive down Delaware's northeastern coast on Delaware Route 9.

The port town of New Castle was founded as a Dutch fort named Casimir in 1651. During the latter part of the seventeenth century, it was fought over and claimed by the Dutch, the Swedes, and finally, the English, who named it

ROUTE 15

From New Castle, follow Delaware Route 9 South. At Thomas Corner, turn right on Road 424, then right on Delaware Route 299. Take Route 299 into Odessa. From Odessa, backtrack on Route 299 and turn right on Route 9 South. Turn left on Road 83 at Dutch Neck Crossroads. Turn right on Road 329 and then left on Road 85 to Bombay Hook National Wildlife Refuge.

ABOVE: *A flock of snow geese lifts off from a pond at Bombay Hook National Wildlife Refuge just after sunrise.*

OPPOSITE, TOP: *Jessop's Tavern is a popular eatery in historic New Castle. Its early eighteenth-century structure was built by Abraham Jessop, a colonial barrel maker.*

OPPOSITE, BOTTOM LEFT: *The cupola atop the 1732 courthouse in New Castle served as the center of the twelve-mile radial circle that formed Delaware's northern boundary with Pennsylvania.*

OPPOSITE, BOTTOM RIGHT: *A statue of William Penn stands in New Castle, where he first landed in America in 1682.*

New Castle and made it the seat of regional government. In 1704, Delaware broke away from Pennsylvania to establish itself as a separate colony, and New Castle was named its capital. In 1776, Delaware adopted a constitution and became the first of all the colonies to call itself a state; New Castle became the state capital.

As a capital city and also an important stop on the north-south trade route, New Castle prospered. The city attracted lawyers, legislators, and other professionals who built large homes in the town. But the capital moved to Dover in 1777, and in 1881, the county seat moved to Wilmington. New Castle was also bypassed by the Chesapeake & Delaware Canal, which ran far south of the city, and long-distance rail lines that connected Baltimore and Philadelphia were laid through Wilmington. The once-thriving New Castle fell asleep.

New Castle's economic decline prevented residents from making major alterations to their homes, and consequently, the structures remained virtually untouched over the years. Today, while revitalized, New Castle looks very much as it did in the eighteenth and nineteenth centuries, complete with brick sidewalks and cobblestone streets. It's like Virginia's Colonial Williamsburg, except that New Castle is a real town. Shops, restaurants, and inns mingle with private homes. Historic structures surround The Green, a common area laid out in 1655, which served as pasture for early residents' livestock. The town's centerpiece is the handsome courthouse, where flags of the Netherlands, Sweden, Great Britain, and the United States proclaim the town's proud heritage. Built in 1732, it was Delaware's first courthouse.

With a copy of the "New Castle Heritage Trail Map" as your guide, you can easily enjoy this small jewel of a town on foot.

Delaware City was originally founded as Newbold's Landing in 1801. The town got its present name of Delaware City in 1826, when the Chesapeake & Delaware Canal was being built. Located on the Delaware River at the eastern entrance of the canal, the town prospered as a major port and commercial center until the advent of the railroad reduced canal traffic. In 1919, the federal government bought the struggling canal company, converted the canal to a sea-level waterway, and moved its eastern entrance two miles south of town. The original canal was converted to a branch channel for pleasure craft.

Today, Delaware City retains much of its nineteenth-century appearance. At the riverfront, you can view the original canal's restored stone-walled lock, which dates back to 1829, and enjoy a lovely view of the river. You can also board a ferry for the short ride to Fort Delaware State Park on Pea Patch Island in the Delaware River. Originally constructed in 1819 to protect the ports of Wilmington and Philadelphia, the fort served as a prison for thousands of Confederate soldiers during the Civil War. When you arrive, costumed historic interpreters transport you back to the summer of 1863 to relive a typical day at the fort.

Pea Patch Island's marshland provides the perfect habitat for one of the largest wading-bird nesting areas on the East Coast. Many of the nine species of herons, egrets, and ibises that reside here can be spotted from a 3/4-mile nature trail.

Just south of Delaware City is another small state park, Fort Du Pont. This former military base encompasses 322 acres along the Delaware River and is a perfect spot for picnicking or fishing.

Back on Route 9, cross over the canal and proceed through the low-lying marshland that is part of the Augustine Wildlife Area. At the tiny fishing hamlet of Port Penn, an interpretive center contains interesting exhibits about the folk life of the wetland communities along the shores of the Delaware River.

Your route now detours to the beautifully preserved village of Odessa, another busy colonial grain-shipping port that met the end of its glory days in the late 1800s. The Du Pont family became enamored with the town's lovely Colonial and Federal architecture, and they used a property here as a retreat. The family's Winterthur Museum acquired five structures in the town and established them as the Historic Houses of Odessa. Dedicated to preserving the architectural heritage of the area's colonial past, the houses are filled with a collection of more than four thousand objects of regional decorative arts for the period ranging from 1760 through 1850.

From Odessa, continue south on Route 9 through the lush marshlands of the Cedar Swamp and Woodland Beach Wildlife areas, where herons, egrets, and other wading birds can be spotted fishing along the creeks. A detour off of Route 9 brings you to the Bombay Hook National Wildlife Refuge.

Established in 1937, the refuge encompasses 16,000 acres of freshwater pools, timbered swamp, grassy upland, and one of the largest nearly unaltered salt marshes in the Mid-Atlantic. It is an important stopover for migrating waterfowl.

Bombay Hook includes a twelve-mile auto tour loop, five nature trails, and three observation towers from which to view the wildlife, which includes some 278 identified bird species, as well as 35 species of mammals. The best opportunities for viewing large numbers of wildlife come during the spring and fall migrations.

An ideal time to visit Bombay Hook is in late fall during the snow goose migration. Up to one hundred thousand geese may be present here during the peak, which is generally around the first week of November. The geese leave the refuge during the day to feed in nearby farm fields. If you arrive around sunrise, you may witness their departure—one of our all-time favorite wildlife experiences. Silence may greet you when you first exit your car, but have patience. Soon you'll hear the faint sounds of what we call "goose chatter." The chatter intensifies, grows louder and louder, and then suddenly, with a great burst of commotion, hundreds of snow geese lift off in unison from a nearby pond. The sky fills with birds. Their raucous honking and frenzied wing flapping creates a symphony of sound unlike anything you've ever heard. The noisy ensemble heads out over the refuge, possibly directly over your head. Then all is quiet once more—until another flock readies for takeoff.

Now a state park, Fort Delaware was originally built on Pea Patch Island in 1819 to protect the ports of Wilmington and Philadelphia. This aerial view shows the remains of a sea wall, which is visible in the foreground and right of the image. Courtesy Library of Congress, Prints & Photographs Division

ABOVE: *A schooner passes a breakwater at Herring Point in Henlopen State Park.*

OPPOSITE PAGE: *Viewed from the shores of Cape Henlopen State Park, the soft pink light of dusk envelopes the Delaware Breakwater East End Lighthouse located in Delaware Bay.*

Sunset light reflects from The Emlen Physick Estate in Cape May. Completed in 1879, it is now home to the Mid-Atlantic Center for the Arts.

ROUTE 16

From Milton, take Delaware Route 16 to Prime Hook National Wildlife Refuge. Backtrack on Route 16 to Milton, and turn left on Union Street. Turn right on Federal Street, then left on Wharton Street, and continue straight; the road becomes Atlantic Street and then Cave Neck Road. Follow Cave Neck Road to Delaware Route 1 (Coastal Highway) and turn right. Take a left onto New Road, and turn right on Pilot Town Road in Lewes. From Lewes, take Cape Henlopen Drive to the Cape May–Lewes Ferry terminal. Cross the Delaware Bay on the ferry. Proceed from the Cape May ferry terminal on U.S. Highway 9, and turn right on Seashore Drive to the town of Cape May.

Lewes, Delaware, and Cape May, New Jersey, are two charming and historic towns separated by the waters of the Delaware Bay. Since the Cape May–Lewes Ferry began operating in 1964, it is easy to visit both towns on one trip. The eighty-minute, seventeen-mile boat ride is a highlight in itself.

Start your journey just east of Lewes in Milton, one of Delaware's historic river towns. Located at the mouth of the Broadkill River, Milton was originally settled in the 1600s. The town was the primary shipping center for eastern Sussex County during the eighteenth and nineteenth centuries. Milton boasts 198 homes listed on the National Register, and its collection of nineteenth-century architecture is one of the finest in the country.

After perusing Milton's historic district, venture a few miles northeast of town to the Prime Hook National Wildlife Refuge. Established in 1963, Prime Hook's mix of wetlands, uplands, and forest provides refuge for a diverse population of birds, fish, and mammals, including the endangered Delmarva Peninsula fox squirrel. The visitors' center has literature and up-to-date information about the best places to spot wildlife at the time of your visit. In fall and spring, many of the migrating species are found on the two large impoundments located along Broadkill Beach Road.

After returning to Milton, quiet backroads lead through Sussex County farmland on the way to Lewes.

Located on the Delaware Bay, Lewes (pronounced loo-iss) is a quiet and pleasant town brimming with upscale shops, restaurants, and inns. There is a public beach and a picturesque harbor from which sport fishing expeditions and whale-watching cruises depart.

Lewes has a long and interesting history. Henry Hudson first explored the area in 1609, while on an expedition for the Dutch East India Company. In 1631, the Dutch established a whaling station here and named it Zwaanendael, which means "valley of the swans." This was the first settlement in present-day Delaware, earning Lewes the title of "the first town in the first state." Unfortunately, less than a year later, local Lenni Lanape Indians massacred all thirty-two settlers after a dispute over a Dutch coat of arms that the settlers had mounted on their settlement.

The area alternated between Dutch and English control until 1673, when the English took control for good. In 1682, the town was named Lewes in honor of a town in Sussex County, England.

Pirates were frequent visitors to Lewes, including the famous Captain Kidd. According to legend, Kidd buried a chest of gold and other treasures among the area's sand dunes. No evidence of it has been found to date.

In 1813, during the War of 1812, a British frigate bombarded Lewes. However, the only casualties were a dead chicken and a pig that suffered a broken leg. In one of the town's historic houses, an embedded cannonball serves as a lingering reminder.

Stop by the visitors' bureau for a walking tour map of the Lewes Historic District. In an effort to preserve the character of Old Lewes, the Lewes

Historical Society maintains a complex of restored structures, dating from the late 1600s and 1700s, that were moved to the site from other locations, including a blacksmith shop, a doctor's office, and a country store.

East of town, Cape Henlopen is perched at the mouth of the Delaware Bay. When these lands were granted to William Penn in 1682, he declared that Cape Henlopen and all of its resources were to be made available for the common usage of the citizens of Lewes and Sussex County. Thus, it became one of the nation's first "public lands."

The cape's strategic location made it the chosen site of Fort Miles, a World War II army base, where bunkers and gun emplacements were camouflaged among the dunes and concrete observation towers were built to spot enemy ships. In 1964, the state of Delaware took control of the property and established the Cape Henlopen State Park.

The park offers a wide variety of activities, including fishing, swimming, canoeing, bird watching, camping, hiking, picnicking, and ranger-led programs. Panoramic views can be enjoyed from one of the old observation towers, now open to the public. From the cape's beaches, you can witness beautiful sunrises over the Atlantic Ocean and sunsets over Delaware Bay.

Next, drive aboard the Cape May–Lewes Ferry for an enjoyable eighty-minute cruise across the Delaware Bay. On board, you will find a lounge, gift shops, and plenty of outside seating where you can sit back and enjoy the views and fresh air. When you exit the ferry, make your way into beautiful Cape May.

Located at the southernmost tip of New Jersey, Cape May is known as "America's first and oldest seashore resort." The city has been welcoming visitors for more than a century, and it has been named a National Historic Landmark. Cape May has more than six hundred authentically restored and preserved Victorian structures dating from between 1850 and 1910.

In 1623, the Dutch explorer Captain Cornelius Jacobson Mey led a flotilla of three ships around the cape. He named it Cape Mey (later changed to May by the English), although he never came ashore. The town was originally established as a whaling settlement around 1648; the residents later turned to agriculture and fishing when the whaling industry declined.

In the early 1800s, steamship service on the Delaware River began transporting tourists from Philadelphia to Cape May, followed soon by railroad service. Scores of people, weary from the big city summer heat, would seek relief at the cool, sandy beaches of Cape May.

You can fill an entire day with a walking tour of this enchanting town. Lovely pastel-colored Victorian homes and inns, decorated with gingerbread trim, line the tree-shaded streets. In the evening, gas lamps add to its old-time charm. A seaside promenade makes a delightful place for an early morning walk. Of course, there are plenty of fine restaurants, quaint bed and breakfasts, and great shops to peruse.

Cape May Point State Park encompasses 190 acres of freshwater wetlands adjacent to the Atlantic, with two miles of nature trails and ample bird watching opportunities. The centerpiece of the park is the historic Cape May Point Lighthouse, which was built in 1859. Visitors are welcome to climb to the top for a spectacular view of the ocean and surrounding Cape May County.

The beaches of Cape May were a lively and popular summer attraction in the early 1900s, as shown in this vintage postcard. From the Voyageur Press Collection

PART V

HISTORIC CHESAPEAKE

ABOVE: *These freshly harvested Chesapeake Bay blue crabs will be on tonight's menu at local restaurants.*

FACING PAGE: *Built in 1827, the 36-foot-tall Concord Point Lighthouse is the centerpiece of Havre de Grace's waterfront.*

Maryland's Tidewater is divided by the great Chesapeake Bay into the relatively higher elevations of its Western Shore (also known as southern Maryland) and the low-lying Eastern Shore, which occupies the Delmarva Peninsula.

The first English colonists settled the newly established colony in 1634. Since then, the Chesapeake Bay has been the heart and soul of Maryland's Tidewater; it dominates nearly every facet of life here. In Colonial days, cities and towns were established along the bay or the waterways that flowed into it. Many became important port towns with bustling harbors full of ferries and cargo vessels. Wagons loaded with tobacco, the colony's main cash crop, were hauled into the ports from nearby farms and plantations for shipment back to Mother England.

In other towns along the bay, residents made their living from the bounty of its waters. Watermen harvested millions of tons of its seafood, including oysters, clams, rockfish, and those famous Chesapeake Bay blue crabs. Seafood houses and canneries were built to process the harvest for an ever-expanding market. A shipbuilding and repair industry grew to meet the increasing demands for more fishing vessels.

After the Revolutionary War, most of the bay's busy ports closed from lack of business. In addition, years of over harvesting led to a severe decline in the available seafood. In turn, many of the seafood processing plants closed, along with the associated shipbuilding and commercial fishing operations.

Today, a journey through Maryland's Chesapeake country reveals small towns and quiet villages that proudly celebrate their colorful past. Early American history abounds with colonial settlements, Revolutionary War and War of 1812 sites, tobacco plantations, canal towns, and weathered fishing villages—all awaiting curious travelers.

In this chapter, you will travel through countryside that is still largely rural with acres of flat farm fields planted with corn, soybeans, and tobacco. Along the way, you'll encounter old mills, one-room schoolhouses, picturesque lighthouses, and lovely historic churches with seventeenth century graveyards. There are quaint port towns with lovingly restored historic centers. The region's parks and natural areas showcase breathtaking scenery and bountiful wildlife, while also providing a playground for water-sport enthusiasts.

THE HEAD OF THE BAY

Skirting along the head of the Chesapeake Bay, this route explores historic towns that were settled early in the nation's history along the rivers that flow into the Upper Bay.

The small town of North East is situated at the mouth of the North East River, which played a major role in the town's settlement in the seventeenth century. By 1710, various mills had been built in the area. In 1735, a group of British businessmen established an iron works called the Principio Company near the town. George Washington's father and brother held an interest in the company, which was later known as the North East Forge.

ROUTE 17

From North East, take Maryland Route 272 south to Turkey Point. From Turkey Point, backtrack north to North East and turn left on Maryland Route 7. Turn left on Maryland Route 267 to Charlestown. Leave Charlestown on Baltimore Street (Route 267), turn left on Carpenters Point Road, right on Mountain Hill Road, and left on Route 7 toward Perryville, where the road becomes Broad Street. Depart Perryville via Mill Creek Road. Turn left on U.S. Highway 40 West, and cross the Susquehanna River to Harve de Grace. After exploring Harve de Grace, take Maryland Route 155 to Earlton Road. Take a right on Earlton Road, then another right on Webster-Lapidum Road. Go left on Quaker Bottom Road and right on Rock Run Road to Susquehanna State Park.

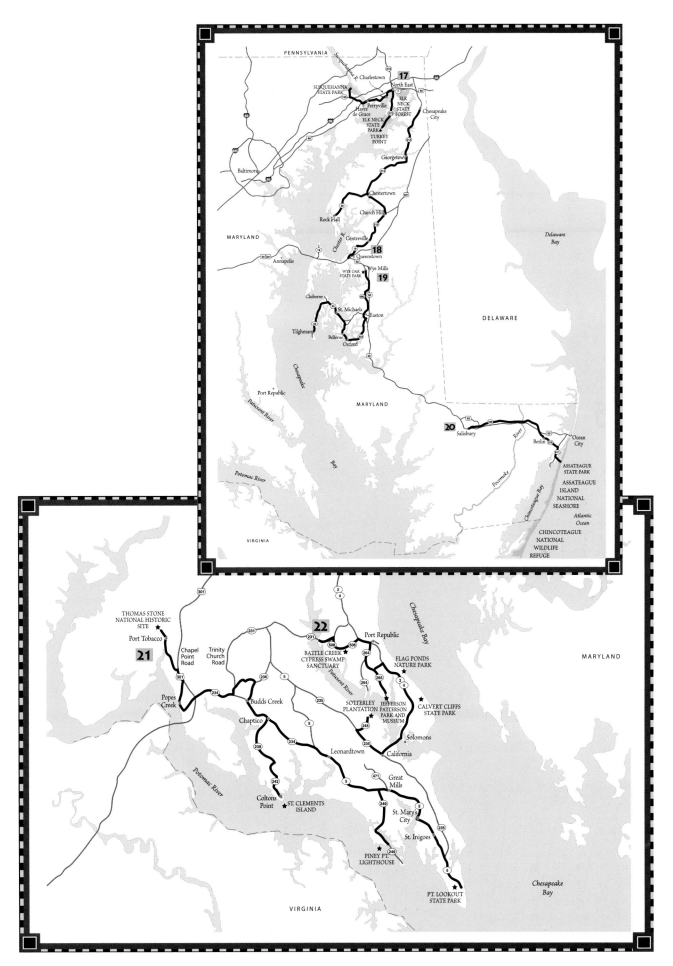

ABOVE: *Perry Point in Perryville offers a grand view of Havre de Grace across the Susquehanna River.*

RIGHT: *A child tosses bread to eager seagulls along Havre de Grace's boardwalk promenade.*

LEFT: *The elegant Victorian Spencer Silver Mansion Bed and Breakfast in Havre de Grace was built in 1896 for merchant and foundry owner John Spencer.*

BELOW: *The Jersey Toll House once served a covered bridge that crossed the Susquehanna River here. It is part of the Rock Run Historic Area in Susquehanna State Park.*

Several historic structures grace North East, including the St. Mary Anne's Episcopal Church. Although the church was established in 1706, the current church building was constructed in 1743 after the original structure had burned down. The graveyard, one of the state's oldest, contains the graves of Susquehannock Indians from the 1600s.

From North East, travel south down the long, hilly peninsula of Elk Neck. You pass through the Elk Neck State Forest on the way to Elk Neck State Park, which is at the end of the peninsula. With 2,188 acres of waterfront forest, this park offers a variety of recreational pursuits such as hiking, swimming, camping, and boating.

The road ends in the parking area at Turkey Point. From there, an easy trail leads to the Turkey Point Lighthouse. This picturesque lighthouse was built in 1834 to guide ships into the Chesapeake & Delaware Canal. It stands on a bluff that is about one hundred feet above the Elk and North East Rivers, where they flow into the Upper Chesapeake Bay.

Return to North East, and take Maryland Route 7 toward Charlestown. Founded as a North East River port in 1742, Charlestown was a major supply depot for the Continental Army during the Revolutionary War. The town's waterfront has four marinas and includes a reproduction of its original eighteenth-century wharf. The Historic District holds 175 structures, many of which date from the Colonial period.

The town of Perryville was first settled in the 1600s when Lord Baltimore granted 31,000 acres of land to George Talbot. Broad Street (Route 7) in Perryville leads to the Susquehanna River and the former site of the Susquehanna Lower Ferry. Established in 1695, the ferry transported passengers between Perryville and Havre de Grace. Travelers on the old Post Road (now U.S. Highway 40), which ran from Baltimore to Philadelphia, crossed the river here. After their ferry ride, they could stop at Rodgers Tavern in Perryville for lodging or a meal.

During the Revolutionary War, Perryville served as a staging area for the Continental Army. Perryville's Rodgers Tavern (built circa 1745) was a favorite stopping place for George Washington, Lafayette, and Rochambeau. The old ferry route became obsolete with the building of bridges and railroads across the Susquehanna in the 1800s, and the tavern ceased operation in 1886. Fortunately, the structure was saved from demolition and restored. It is owned by the Town of Perryville and is open to the public.

Behind the tavern, a path leads to Perry Point, which offers a marvelous view of Havre de Grace across the Susquehanna. To get to that lovely town, leave Perryville on U.S. 40 and cross the mighty river on the Thomas J. Hatem Memorial Bridge.

In 1658, a settler named Godfrey Harmer purchased 200 acres of land, which he called Harmer's Town. That tract makes up the heart of the Historic District in today's Havre de Grace. Perched at the mouth of the Susquehanna where the river flows into the Chesapeake Bay, the picturesque town got its name from the Marquis de Lafayette. The French general and diplomat visited the town in 1782, and he was impressed by its resemblance to the seaport of

Le Havre in France. He suggested Havre de Grace (Harbor of Grace) for the town's name. In 1785, the citizens incorporated the City of Havre de Grace. In 1789, it was considered as the location for the nation's capital, but it lost the title to Washington, D.C., by one vote.

In May of 1813, during the War of 1812, British forces attacked the town and nearly burned it to the ground. Reportedly, just two houses and a church were spared the carnage.

Havre de Grace became a vital commercial intersection when the Susquehanna & Tidewater Canal was completed in 1840. The canal stretched forty-five miles from Havre de Grace to Wrightsville, Pennsylvania, and opened central Pennsylvania to trade between Baltimore and Philadelphia. The canal was shut down in 1900 due to railroad competition. This period in the town's history is explained through interesting exhibits at the Susquehanna Museum of Havre de Grace in the canal's restored lock house.

A new railroad bridge was constructed in 1866 to link Havre de Grace and Perryville across the Susquehanna. Courtesy Library of Congress, Prints & Photographs Division

Havre de Grace has an alluring array of inns, restaurants, antique shops, galleries, and boutiques. Its beautiful waterfront includes a boardwalk promenade that winds along the bay. The centerpiece of the waterfront is the 1827 Concord Point Lighthouse, the second-oldest lighthouse on the Chesapeake Bay. The skipjack *Martha Lewis* is one of the last remaining working dredge boats that make up the Chesapeake Bay oyster fleet. It is docked at the waterfront in Tydings Park.

From Havre de Grace, drive a few miles west of town to the Steppingstone Farm Museum, located within the Susquehanna State Park. This private, not-for-profit museum (open weekends from May through October) strives to preserve the rural arts and crafts of the 1880–1920 period in Harford County. The farmhouse, shops, and barn are located on the site of a former working farm.

Continue from the farm to the main recreational area of the Susquehanna State Park, where there is a campground, boat launch, hiking and mountain biking trails, and picnic areas. Direct access to the river provides excellent fishing opportunities.

The remains of a once-thriving commercial center are located in the park's Rock Run Historic Area. It includes the restored and fully operational Rock Run Grist Mill, built in 1794; a section of the Susquehanna & Tidewater Canal; a miller's house; and the Jersey Toll House, where tolls were collected for a covered bridge that once crossed the Susquehanna here. The Rock Run House overlooks the mill from its hillside perch. The fourteen-room stone mansion was built in 1804 by John Carter, one of the mill's partners.

The historic sailing ship Kalmar Nyckel *is illuminated in port during Chestertown's annual Downrigging Weekend.*

LEFT: *Chestertown's Downrigging Weekend provides opportunities for close-up inspections of the many historic sailing vessels docked in the harbor.*

BELOW: *Fishermen unload their catch of Chesapeake Bay blue crabs at the docks in Rock Hall harbor.*

CHESAPEAKE BAY FACTS

The Chesapeake Bay's name came from the Algonquian word *Chesepiooc*, meaning "great shellfish bay." When Captain John Smith explored and mapped out the great bay from 1607 to 1609, he found waters filled with seafood, including blue crabs, clams, and oysters.

The Chesapeake Bay is the largest estuary (where salt and freshwater mix) in the United States. It stretches about 200 miles from Havre de Grace, Maryland, to Norfolk, Virginia. Its width ranges from just 3.4 miles near Aberdeen, Maryland, to 35 miles near the mouth of the Potomac.

The area of the bay and its tidal tributaries is 4,480 square miles, with 11,684 miles of shoreline. Given the large surface area, it is surprisingly shallow with an average depth of just 21 feet.

The Chesapeake Bay holds more than 18 trillion gallons of water. Half of that water comes from the Atlantic and the rest drains from some 150 rivers and streams in its 64,000-square-mile watershed, which includes the District of Columbia and parts of Delaware, Maryland, New York, Pennsylvania, Virginia, and West Virginia. Its largest river source is the Susquehanna, which provides about fifty percent of the bay's freshwater.

The bay is home to twenty-nine species of waterfowl and it is a major stop along the Atlantic Flyway. It supports more than 3,600 species of plants, fish, and animals.

More than 15 million people live in the bay's watershed. Runoff from urban areas and farms presents a major threat to the health and productivity of its waters, as do over harvesting and the invasion of foreign species. Even so, with a harvest of 500 million pounds of seafood per year, the Chesapeake Bay still yields more than any other United States estuary.

This map of Virginia and the Chesapeake Bay was prepared in the early seventeenth century based on the explorations of Captain John Smith. Courtesy Library of Congress, Prints & Photographs Division

ABOVE THE BRIDGE

ROUTE 18

From Queenstown, follow Maryland Route 18 to Centreville. Turn left on Maryland Route 213 and proceed to Chesapeake City. At Chestertown, a side trip west on Maryland Route 20 leads to Rock Hall.

The Chesapeake Bay Bridge crosses the great bay at one of its narrowest points. Just over four miles of bridge separates the megalopolis of Baltimore, Washington, and Annapolis from Maryland's Eastern Shore. Yet, that distance could just as easily be four thousand miles, because crossing that bridge is like entering a different world. The quiet countryside of the Eastern Shore bears no resemblance to the throbbing urban complex on the other side of the bay. In fact, its largest "city" has fewer than thirty thousand inhabitants.

Heading northward from the east end of the bridge, you will see miles of flat, fertile fields of wheat, corn, and soybeans in the still largely agricultural area that occupies the northwestern portion of the Delmarva Peninsula. This region has been farmed, hunted, and fished for thousands of years, first by Native Americans, and then by colonists who filled its fields with tobacco. Tobacco was such an important cash crop in the 1700s that it was used as currency; the prices for goods were quoted in pounds of tobacco.

The tobacco, grain, and other commodities were shipped out of busy port towns that grew up along the Chester, Sassafras, and Bohemia Rivers. Steamboats also frequented the ports and transported human cargo from place to place. Today, these historic towns and villages provide many interesting highlights for travelers and tourists.

The tour begins in the village of Queenstown, the original county seat of Queen Anne's County. Queenstown was established in 1707 and became a significant shipping port in the eighteenth century. Local planters exported their tobacco and grain to Mother England and imported her manufactured goods through this busy port on the Chester River. The original (restored) county courthouse, built in 1709, still stands proudly in the center of the historic little village.

In 1782, the county seat moved to a more central part of the county to a town that was appropriately renamed Centreville. The courthouse, which was constructed in 1792, is Maryland's oldest still in continuous use. Situated on the town square and surrounded by tall, beautiful shade trees and boxwood hedges, the lovely old building is the centerpiece of Centreville. A bronze statue of Queen Anne, for whom the county was named, adorns the front lawn.

At one time, the tiny hamlet of Church Hill had as many as six churches, but its name most likely came from the beautiful St. Luke's Episcopal Church, which was known as "the church on the hill." St. Luke's is one of the oldest churches in the state that is still in its original structure. The church was built in 1732 at a cost of 140,000 pounds of tobacco. During the Civil War, Federal troops reportedly used the old church as a barracks.

Just over the county line in Kent County, Chestertown was an important colonial Mid-Atlantic port town on the Chester River. It was a prosperous shipbuilding and trading center during the eighteenth and nineteenth centuries. The town, which celebrated its three hundredth birthday in 2006, is known for its patriotic acts during the American Revolution. Its citizens staged their own version of the Boston Tea Party on May 23, 1774. After hearing that the British had closed the Port of Boston, angry residents climbed on board the British brigantine *Geddes*, which was anchored in the Chester, and defiantly tossed its cargo of tea overboard. (A re-enactment of this daring Chestertown Tea Party is staged every Memorial Day weekend.) As an expression of gratitude for this and other acts of support during the war, George Washington contributed fifty guineas and his name to the founding of Washington College in 1782. Washington College is the nation's tenth-oldest liberal arts college.

Chestertown today is a delightful place to visit. The historic downtown and waterfront is abuzz with activity. Specialty shops, antique stores, galleries, eateries, and theaters are located along the wide, shady streets. A town square, complete with an antique fountain, is the location for concerts and other festivities. Boats, including the schooner *Sultana*, ply the Chester River. They sail past grand and stately homes that were built by wealthy eighteenth- and nineteenth-century merchants.

ABOVE: *Eclectic shops, art galleries, antique stores, and eateries line the streets of downtown Chestertown.*

RIGHT: *A bronze statue of Good Queen Anne graces the lawn in front of the 1792 Queen Anne County Courthouse in Centreville.*

OPPOSITE PAGE: *Now a museum, the 1885 Little Red Schoolhouse near Easton is the only one-room schoolhouse remaining in Talbot County.*

A side trip from Chestertown travels to the bay-front village of Rock Hall, widely known as the "pleasure boating center of the Upper Eastern Shore." Visitors flock to Rock Hall, many by boat, to enjoy all of the little town's attractions, including a Waterman's Museum, antique and curio shops, artisans and crafters, an old-fashioned ice cream parlor, and seafood restaurants. The town and its many marinas are hopping with activity from spring through fall.

Georgetown, located on the Sassafras River, was another important port of entry and ferry landing in the eighteenth century. It also served as a supply base for the Continental Army from 1775 through 1783. During the War of 1812, the British burned the town. Only a church and two brick houses were left standing, which survived by virtue of the heroic act of "Kitty" Knight. Refusing to leave her invalid neighbor, Miss Knight defiantly told the British, "I shall not leave. If you burn this house, you burn me with it."

Past Georgetown, you drive through the rich farmland of Cecil County toward Chesapeake City. This picturesque and inviting town was once known as the "Village of Bohemia." It prospered with the 1829 completion of the Chesapeake & Delaware (C&D) Canal, which connected the Delaware River with the Chesapeake Bay and the Port of Baltimore. Huge commercial vessels and pleasure boats still pass through the canal, which is the busiest in the nation. The town itself has much to offer with attractive nineteenth-century architecture, wonderful waterfront restaurants, interesting shops, and tours of the canal and its museum.

The Chesapeake Bay and the many tributaries that feed into it have played heavily in the history of the Eastern Shore. You are never far from water on this trip. The tidal shore's marshes, reeds, and rushes provide the perfect habitat for a wide range of birds and waterfowl. Depending on the season, frequent sightings of geese, herons, egrets, ospreys, or other winged creatures can be anticipated. The estuarine habitat, where salt and fresh water meet, produces a rich variety of fish species. Fishermen flock to the region to harvest the bounty, especially the prized striped bass that is known locally as "rockfish."

BELOW THE BRIDGE

ROUTE 19

From Wye Mills, take Maryland Route 662 south. Turn right on U.S. Highway 50, then take a right to rejoin Route 662, and proceed to Easton. From Easton, follow Maryland Route 333 to Oxford. Cross the Tred Avon River via the Bellevue-Oxford Ferry and continue north on Bellevue Road. Turn left on Maryland Route 329, then left on Maryland Route 33 to St. Michaels. Continue on Route 33 from St. Michaels. Just west of St. Michaels, near McDaniel, a side trip on Maryland Route 451 leads to Claiborne. Return to Route 33 to proceed to Tilghman.

If you head south after crossing the Chesapeake Bay Bridge into Maryland's Eastern Shore, you hit Talbot County, the "Crown of the Chesapeake Bay." Famous for pleasure boating, sumptuous seafood, and gorgeous sunsets, Talbot also has a rich history dating to the seventeenth century.

The first stop, Wye Mills, is one of Maryland's oldest communities. By 1706, three mills were in operation on the Wye River, and the little village had earned its name of Wye Mills. One of the first gristmills was built in 1682, and it continues to operate today as a working museum. It is the oldest frame gristmill on the Eastern Shore and one of the earliest industrial sites in the state. During the Revolutionary War, Wye Mill flour went to feed Washington's army at Valley Forge.

Nearby is the site of the Wye oak, the former centerpiece of the Wye Oak State Park. In 2002, a storm's sixty-mile-per-hour winds toppled the magnificent

95-foot tall, 460-year old tree, which had been documented as the largest white oak tree in the eastern United States. A restored early nineteenth-century schoolhouse is located near the tree's remains, and the Old Wye Church (circa 1721), one of the nation's oldest Episcopal churches, is farther down the road.

Past the church, watch for Orrell's Maryland Beaten Biscuits. Ruth Orrell used her mother's recipe for her famous biscuits, which she first sold to the public in 1935. Beaten biscuits originated in southern Maryland and the Eastern Shore during Colonial days, when leavening was scarce. The only way to get biscuit dough to rise was to beat it with a hammer or the back of an axe for half an hour. Today, a special roller has replaced the hammer at Orrell's, but each biscuit is still hand-shaped by ladies sitting around a kitchen table.

This 1936 view of downtown Easton shows a line of brick row houses and businesses along Washington Street. Courtesy Library of Congress, Prints & Photographs Division

Proceeding south, you will pass old country estates and large farms en route to Easton, Talbot's county seat. In 1712, Easton became the "colonial capital of the Eastern Shore" when Maryland's legislature authorized construction of a courthouse in the town. Today, the stately courthouse is the centerpiece of the historic downtown, which is lined with handsome eighteenth- and nineteenth-century buildings that house an eclectic assortment of shops, galleries, and restaurants.

The Quakers were the first Europeans to settle here, in the 1600s. In 1682, they built the Third Haven Friends Meeting House, which still stands on South Washington Street. It is the oldest house of worship that is still in use in the United States, and it is the oldest dated building in Maryland.

From Easton, the drive continues south through Edmundson, Baileys, and Oxford Necks into the village of Oxford. The village was founded as a seaport on the Tred Avon River in 1683. A year later, Oxford and another new town, Anne Arundel (now Annapolis), were named the only two ports of entry for all of Colonial Maryland. The port town was surrounded by wealthy tobacco plantations, and it prospered as an international shipping center until the Revolutionary War. Afterward, Oxford fell into hard times. Wheat had replaced tobacco as a major cash crop, and British ships were no longer bringing imported goods into the village's port.

After the Civil War, the completion of the local railroad and a rising national market for local oysters contributed to another boom for Oxford. Yet, the oyster beds were depleted by the early twentieth century, businesses closed, and Oxford reverted to a quiet waterman's village. It remains a quiet village today, but its idyllic waterside location and historic charm have made it a popular tourist stop.

Throughout the town are attractive eighteenth-century homes and buildings, including the Robert Morris Inn. Robert Morris Jr., son of the inn's original

The Old Wye Church was built in 1721 and is one of the oldest Episcopal churches in the country.

Dating from 1710, the Robert Morris Inn in Oxford is famous for its traditional Chesapeake Bay seafood, particularly its crab cakes.

LEFT: *A boatman at the Chesapeake Bay Maritime Museum's boat yard works on the restoration of a Chesapeake Bay skipjack.*

BELOW: *Fishing boats sit idle in the harbor at Tilghman Island.*

owner, was a signer of the Declaration of Independence, the Articles of Confederation, and the U.S. Constitution. James Michener frequented the inn while researching his book, *Chesapeake,* and he wrote its outline in the inn's tavern—probably while savoring their crab cakes, which he rated as the best on the Eastern Shore.

The historic Oxford-Bellevue Ferry is the nation's oldest privately operated ferry, and it still offers a scenic ten-minute ride across the Tred Avon River to Bellevue. From the Bellevue ferry dock, travel north to connect with Maryland Route 33, the main road into St. Michaels.

Located on the Miles River, St. Michaels is a quaint maritime village with a colorful past. Settled in 1677, it served as a trading post for tobacco farmers and trappers. It later became an important shipbuilding center. During the War of 1812, British marines launched a night attack on the town. Its forewarned residents, hoping to trick the British into firing too high, darkened their houses and hung lanterns in treetops and on ships' masts. The scheme worked and St. Michaels became known as "the town that fooled the British."

The late nineteenth century brought oyster and seafood packing houses and canneries to St. Michaels, most of which are now gone. In their place is a vibrant tourist waterfront that houses one of Maryland's top cultural attractions, the Chesapeake Bay Maritime Museum. The eighteen-acre complex includes a working boat yard and buildings that contain interactive exhibits on Chesapeake Bay life and history. The Hooper Strait Lighthouse, a restored 1879 screw-pile structure, is the museum's centerpiece.

St. Michaels is a joy to visit. Several companies offer boat tours, including romantic sunset sails and nature expeditions. The historic and picturesque town is filled with upscale accommodations and fabulous restaurants. It's a shopper's delight with shops, galleries, and boutiques stocked with unusual items.

On your way from St. Michaels to Tilghman Island, you may want to make a detour up Maryland Route 451 to the site of an old ferry dock at Claiborne. Now a public boat launch, the site is a perfect location to witness a Chesapeake Bay sunset.

The tiny and remote Tilghman Island is perched at the end of the long, narrow peninsula that juts into the Chesapeake Bay like a long, bony finger. The island lacks the refined ambiance of St. Michaels; it's a little crusty and rough around the edges. However, Tilghman is just what you would expect from one of the few remaining authentic, working waterman's villages. Its streets are lined with small, simple houses where boats are the yard ornaments of choice. Vessels of every description move in and out of Tilghman's busy harbors and marinas, and fishermen unload their day's catch on the docks. Much of that bounty ends up in local waterside restaurants, where patrons dine on the freshest seafood possible while enjoying spectacular water views.

A few old oyster dredgers called skipjacks are docked at Dogwood Harbor. The oldest of these is the beautifully restored *Rebecca T. Ruark,* which was built in 1886. It is a National Historic Landmark.

CHESAPEAKE BAY SKIPJACKS

A skipjack is a type of sailboat indigenous to the Chesapeake Bay. The boat was introduced in the 1890s and is thought to be named after a type of fish that skips in and out of the water. The skipjack was designed specifically for the oyster industry. Skipjacks became the preferred oyster dredgers for the Chesapeake Bay watermen, since the boats were inexpensive, easy to build, light, and could be easily navigated in the shallow waters of the bay.

Because of the massive number of oyster dredgers on the bay in the late 1800s and the depletion of the oyster population, a series of conservation laws were passed by Maryland's legislature. One such law forbids oyster dredging by powered vessels, which makes the sail-powered skipjacks America's last commercial sailing fleet.

During the peak of the industry in the 1800s, the annual oyster harvest was around 1.5 million bushels. At that time, there were as many as two thousand skipjacks working the bay. As oyster stocks diminished and legislation increased, however, skipjack captains were left with little profit to maintain their vessels. By 2000, the active dredging fleet had been reduced to about a dozen.

That year, the State of Maryland committed to restore and preserve the Chesapeake Bay fleet because of its historical significance. The skipjack was designated Maryland's official boat, and the state launched a skipjack restoration program with funding provided by the Maryland Historic Trust, the National Trust for Historic Preservation, and numerous private businesses. The restorations are conducted under the direction of the master shipwright at the Chesapeake Bay Maritime Museum, with labor supplied by a crew of boat carpenter apprentices.

A number of these vessels have already been restored and can be found in harbors around the Bay, including Tilghman Island and Havre de Grace.

In the early 1900s, skipjacks were a familiar site on the waters of the Chesapeake Bay. Courtesy the Mariners' Museum, Newport News, VA

WILD PONIES AMONG THE DUNES

The key factor in the establishment and subsequent growth of Salisbury, the largest city on Maryland's Eastern Shore, was its location. Salisbury is situated at the headwaters of the Wicomico River, a navigable waterway that flows to the Chesapeake Bay. The city was founded in 1732 as a port city, and it became a gateway for colonists seeking land for homesteading. Due to its deep, wide channel that enables huge tankers and barges to pass through, Salisbury is second only to Baltimore as Maryland's most active port. With its location near the center of the Delmarva Peninsula, the city also developed into a major commercial crossroads. Sitting at the intersection of main highway and railway lines, it became known as the "hub of the Eastern Shore."

There are many things to see and do in Salisbury. The Newtown Historic District features lovely Federal, Victorian, and Colonial-style homes. It is the oldest residential neighborhood in the city and the first to be rebuilt after a

ROUTE 20

From Salisbury, take Maryland Route 346 East (Old Ocean City Road) to Berlin. From Berlin, take Maryland Route 376 (Bay Street/Assateague Road) east. Turn right on Maryland Route 611 and proceed to Assateague Island National Seashore.

The sun sets over Chincoteague Bay at Assateague Island National Seashore.

Fights can sometimes break out among the wild horses on Assateague Island.

A great blue heron fishes for breakfast at Assateague Island National Seashore.

devastating fire in 1886 nearly burned the city to the ground. The Downtown Plaza Historic District contains a pleasant tree-lined pedestrian mall with historic buildings and a variety of shops, galleries, and restaurants. The Salisbury Zoo houses nearly four hundred animals inside natural habitats and has been called one of the finest small zoos in the East. The Pemberton Historical Park is part of a former plantation situated along the Wicomico River. It contains the 1741 Pemberton Hall manor house, as well as 4.5 miles of nature trails that wind through the surrounding wetlands, forests, and meadows.

These days, most of the traffic heading east from Salisbury to Ocean City follows the larger and faster U.S. Highway 50, the Ocean Gateway. If you're looking for a slower, more relaxed pace, take Old Ocean City Road (Maryland Route 346), which cuts through flat farmland and sleepy rural villages and crosses over the Pocomoke, a state-designated Wild and Scenic Black Water River.

Soon you will arrive at the pretty little town of Berlin (pronounced BUR-lin), which was founded in the 1790s. Berlin's Main Street was once the old Philadelphia Post Road, the main colonial route that connected commerce centers to the north and west. Travelers would stop at the Burleigh Inn, a tavern that was probably the source of the town's name. (Most believe the name came about as a contraction of "Burleigh" and "Inn.")

Berlin residents have done a beautiful job of restoring their town center as well as maintaining and preserving their historic commercial and residential districts. The area contains an impressive number of structures that date from the Federal and Victorian periods. The Victorian town center and lovely old homes are set along shady streets lined with magnolia, sycamore, and gingko trees. It gives you the feeling that you've stepped back in time to another era.

There is a walking tour of the town, a museum, and a number of shopping and dining opportunities. Be sure to check out the Atlantic Hotel, a gracious Victorian inn that was built in 1895. Actor Richard Gere stayed at this beautifully restored hotel while shooting the film *Runaway Bride* with Julia Roberts. As the filming location for the 1998 movie, Berlin's streets were transformed into the fictional town of Hale, Maryland.

From Berlin, leave the Old Ocean City Road behind and head southeast toward the Atlantic Ocean and Assateague Island, the final stop of this tour.

Assateague is bordered by the Atlantic on the east and the Sinepuxent and Chincoteague Bays on the west. The name, which means "a running stream between," comes from the name of a local Indian tribe. This is a barrier island that was built from sand raised from the ocean floor by the persistent motion of waves over time. Because Assateague Island is composed entirely of sand, its shape and size is constantly changing, thanks to the forces of wind and water. Before 1933, it was attached to Ocean City as a part of the long peninsula that extends south from Fenwick Island, Delaware. However, a storm during that year created an inlet at Ocean City and severed Assateague from the peninsula, leaving it in its present island form.

Shared by Maryland and Virginia, Assateague is made up of three public areas: Assateague Island National Seashore, managed by the National Park

The Wild Horses of Assateague

A romantic legend relates that on a dark and stormy night in the 1500s, a Spanish galleon wrecked in rough seas off of Assateague Island. A cargo of Spanish mustangs were onboard and managed to escape the ship to swim to the island. Since then, the tough little horses have been roaming wild on Assateague.

Romantic, yes, but not a probable story. The most plausible explanation for the horses' presence is that they descended from domestic stock that were placed on Assateague by seventeenth-century mainland residents trying to avoid fencing laws and livestock taxation.

Whatever their origin, the feral "ponies" do roam free on the island and live primarily on a diet of salt marsh cord grass. The high level of salt in their diet leads them to consume and retain an abnormal volume of water, which accounts for their bloated or pot-bellied appearance.

The horses are split into two herds; there is one in Maryland and one in Virginia. The herds are separated by a fence at the state line. The size of each herd is kept at around 150, in order to limit their impact on the fragile island environment.

Virginia's horses inhabit the Chincoteague National Wildlife Refuge, but they are owned and managed by the Chincoteague Volunteer Fire Department. Each year, the volunteers round up the horses, swim them across the channel into town, and auction many of the foals in an effort to manage the herd's size. In Maryland, a unique contraception method is used. The birth control is administered by dart gun, the program is ninety-five percent effective, and it has no ill side effects.

The shaggy little horses were made popular by Marguerite Henry's children's book, *Misty of Chincoteague*, and they are the stars of Assateague. They're so cute, it's hard to remember that they are wild animals, but they do kick and bite—so keep your distance.

Service; Assateague State Park, managed by the Maryland Department of Natural Resources; and Virginia's Chincoteague National Wildlife Refuge, managed by the U.S. Fish and Wildlife Service. The three agencies work together to provide for the recreational use and enjoyment of the island by the public, while at the same time protecting its natural features and ecosystems.

Unlike Ocean City, its busy northern neighbor, Assateague has no "strip" lined with hotels, restaurants, or amusement parks. Instead, it provides a peaceful and relaxing setting where the only available lodging is in one of three national and state park campgrounds.

An endless array of activities awaits you here; it is guaranteed to rejuvenate your spirit and stimulate your senses. You can hike on short nature trails or along the miles of pristine, undisturbed national seashore beach. You can go swimming, biking, canoeing, surf fishing, clamming, crabbing, or shell collecting.

Even though this is a harsh coastal environment, scores of animals have adjusted to the conditions and make their homes within the island's varied habitats. Birds and waterfowl are plentiful, especially during the spring and fall migrations. Other wildlife you may see includes frogs, toads, turtles, squirrels, fox, and raccoon. Two species of deer inhabit the island: the common white-tailed variety, and the non-native Sika deer, a small species of Asian elk that was introduced here in the 1920s.

The best-known and most adored animals are the small, wild Assateague horses. They roam free and can be spotted almost anywhere, including in the middle of the road, beside your picnic table, or (always a special thrill to see) running wild through the surf.

OPPOSITE, TOP: *Costumed interpreters tend a garden at Historic St. Mary's City, a living history museum located at the site of Maryland's first capital.*

OPPOSITE, BOTTOM: *The charming Cecil's Country Store in Great Mills offers antiques, gifts, and local art.*

RIGHT: *A chair sits on a gravesite in the cemetery of the 1736 Christ Church in Chaptico. It is said that the grave's occupant comes out at night to sit.*

BELOW: *Haberdeventure, meaning "dwelling place in the winds," is the restored 1771 plantation home of Thomas Stone, a prominent Maryland lawyer and signer of the Declaration of Independence.*

ROUTE 21

From Port Tobacco, take Rose Hill Road to Thomas Stone National Historic Site. Return to Port Tobacco and follow Chapel Point Road south. Turn right on U.S. Highway 301, then right on Popes Creek Road to Popes Creek. Continue south on Popes Creek Road, and turn left on Edge Hill Road to U.S. 301. Head north on U.S. 301 (you'll need to turn right, or south, and make a U-turn). Turn right on Maryland Route 234. Turn left on Trinity Church Road, then right Ryceville Road, left on North Ryceville Road, right on Dixie Lyon Road, and right on Maryland Route 236 to Budds Creek. Turn left onto Route 234. For a side trip to Coltons Point, turn right on Maryland Route 238 in Chaptico, and take another right on Maryland Route 242. From Chaptico, continue southeast on Route 234 to Leonardtown. Turn right on Maryland Route 5 toward Great Mills. A side trip south on Maryland Route 249 just prior to Great Mills leads to Piney Point Lighthouse. In Great Mills, turn left on Maryland Route 471 a short distance to reach Cecil's Old Mill. Backtrack to Route 5 and turn left (east) and proceed to St. Mary's City and on to Point Lookout.

A drive through Charles and St. Mary's Counties, the birthplace of the state, is a fascinating exploration of southern Maryland's colonial and wartime history. It is also a relaxing trek through tranquil farmland and small friendly communities. Additionally, this land is surrounded and carved out by the waters of myriad rivers, inlets, and bays, and the miles of shoreline and lush wetlands provide stunning scenery and prime habitat for birds and wildlife.

George Calvert, the first Lord Baltimore, acquired the land through a grant from King Charles I of England, and Calvert resolved to create a new colony based on religious tolerance. On March 25, 1634, the first group of colonists, including Calvert's sons Leonard and George, arrived at St. Clements Island, in present St. Mary's County, aboard two ships, the *Ark* and the *Dove*. The first permanent settlement, at St. Mary's City, was established just twenty-seven years after the founding of Jamestown, which made it the fourth English settlement in the New World.

Evidence of the area's early history is found all along the route, beginning at the Port Tobacco Historic District. Port Tobacco was originally an Indian village, and it is one of the oldest communities on the East Coast. Soon after the Calverts landed at St. Clements Island, Port Tobacco was colonized by the English. It was a busy shipping port and the seat of Charles County until the surrounding farmland became unproductive from years of tobacco farming and the Port Tobacco River silted in, closing its port. After the courthouse burned in 1892, the county seat was moved to La Plata.

Today, the Port Tobacco site has a reconstructed courthouse, an original eighteenth-century home, and a restored one-room schoolhouse. Nearby, the Thomas Stone National Historic Site is the restored plantation home of one of Maryland's four signers of the Declaration of Independence.

On Chapel Point Road, you will pass St. Ignatius, the first of numerous historic churches on this trip. It was founded in 1641 by Rev. Andrew White, who had accompanied the Catholic settlers on board the *Ark* and *Dove*. St. Ignatius is the oldest Catholic parish with a continual pastorate in the country. Inside the current church, which was built in 1798, is a "relic of the true cross" that Father White brought with him from England in 1634. This relic and many others that have come into the possession of various churches throughout the world are believed to be fragmentary remains of the cross upon which Christ was crucified.

When the Protestant Reformation spilled over from Europe into the New World, Maryland's Catholics and other non-Protestants were persecuted—somewhat ironic, considering the colony was founded on the promise of religious tolerance. Reformists captured Father White and another priest and returned them to England as prisoners. For years, Catholics were prohibited from public worship and from holding public office in Maryland.

Although Charles and St. Mary's Counties are laced with colonial sites and sites pertaining to the Revolutionary War and War of 1812, the Civil War also played a prominent role in the area's history. Even though Maryland was a

Constructed in 1785, the St. Ignatius Church in St. Inigoes has its original stained glass windows and an elaborate altar.

Union state, southern Maryland sided largely with the Confederacy since it depended on slave labor to operate the tobacco plantations. After John Wilkes Booth assassinated President Lincoln in April of 1865, he made his escape from Washington through Charles County into Virginia, aided by Maryland Confederate sympathizers. Booth and his accomplice boarded a small boat in the Popes Creek area to cross the Potomac into Virginia. These days, this small community is more happily known for its superb crab houses and stunning Potomac sunsets.

Today, southern Maryland is mostly rural. Miles of flat, open farmland are occasionally interrupted by small towns and a few heavier areas of development. An Amish community of more than two hundred families is concentrated along Maryland Route 236, where farmers work their fields with horse-drawn plows and navigate the roads in horse-drawn buggies. They sell their produce and wares at farmers' markets and roadside stands.

Chaptico, the second oldest community in St. Mary's County, was another important colonial port town on the Wicomico River. Yet, like Port Tobacco, the port closed when the river silted in. The town's lovely Christ Episcopal Church was built in 1736 and still welcomes worshipers today. During the War of 1812, British soldiers raided Chaptico. They used the church to stable their horses among its pews and dug up graves in its cemetery.

A short distance from Chaptico, you may wish to make a side trip south on Route 242 to visit Coltons Point and the St. Clements Island Potomac River Museum, which traces Maryland's history. On weekends in June through October, water taxi tours are available to St. Clements Island, where the colonists first landed in 1634.

The next stop is in Leonardtown, St. Mary's county seat. The little community on Breton Bay is built around a charming town square. Among its interesting historical sites are the Old Town Jail, the grounds of which contain a cannon from the *Ark*, and Tudor Hall, an impressive Georgian mansion that

A boardwalk trail winds through a canopy of trees at the Battle Creek Cypress Swamp Sanctuary in Calvert County.

A swan swims by the Drum Point Lighthouse at dusk in the Calvert Marine Museum in Solomons.

was built around 1744 and was home to Philip Key, uncle of Frances Scott Key.

Next, travel south on Maryland Route 249 to the Piney Point Lighthouse Museum and Park. Built in 1836 and retired in 1964, the lighthouse is the focal point of this small, pleasant park on the Potomac.

In the town of Great Mills, Cecil's Mill Historic District features a mill that was originally constructed around 1810 as a textile factory. Today, it has a working water wheel and other artifacts from its days as the center of this once-thriving industrial district. The historic mill now houses the St. Mary's County Art Association where members exhibit and sell arts and crafts.

Historic St. Mary's City is an outdoor living history museum that is located on the site of the state's first capital. It includes the reconstructed 1676 State House, the Godiah Spray tobacco plantation, an Indian hamlet, fascinating archeological exhibits, and a full-size replica of the *Dove*, one of the two ships that transported the first colonists to Maryland in 1634.

At the end of Maryland Route 5 is Point Lookout State Park. This scenic park sits at the tip of the peninsula and features a retired (and reportedly haunted) lighthouse. You can enjoy a host of aquatic activities on both the Potomac River, on the park's western side, and the Chesapeake Bay on its eastern shores. There is also a museum that chronicles the area's Civil War-era use as a Union prison camp, where as many as twenty thousand Confederate soldiers were imprisoned at one time.

SOUTHERN MARYLAND'S WESTERN SHORE

ROUTE 22

From the Patuxent River Bridge, head east on Maryland Route 231 (Hallowing Point Road). Turn right on Maryland Route 508, then left on Maryland Route 506 to Battle Creek Cypress Swamp Sanctuary. Continue east on Route 506, and turn right on Maryland Route 2/4. Turn right on Maryland Route 264 (Broomes Island Road), then left on Maryland Route 265 (Mackall Road) to Jefferson Patterson Park and Museum. Backtrack on Route 265 and turn right on Parran Road to rejoin Route 2/4. Turn right on Route 2/4. Watch for left turns along Route 2/4 to visit Flag Ponds Nature Park and Calvert Cliffs State Park. Continue south on Route 2/4 to Solomons. Cross the Patuxent River on the Thomas Johnson Memorial Bridge and proceed to California. From California, turn right on Maryland Route 235, then right on Maryland Route 245 to Sotterley Plantation.

Calvert and St. Mary's Counties are part of what is frequently referred to as the Western Shore because they occupy the state's western shores of the mighty Chesapeake Bay. Calvert County, named for founder George Calvert, sits on a narrow peninsula that is surrounded by the waters of the great bay on the east and the Patuxent River on the west. The area remains largely rural. As you follow this route, you will encounter eighteenth-century churches and restored one-room schoolhouses, country markets, and antique stores. In season, produce from the area's numerous farms can be purchased at roadside stands.

Begin your journey on the eastern banks of the Patuxent on Maryland Route 231, which is also called Hallowing Point Road. This was the site of a steamboat landing, and the area received its name from people hollering for the ferry to stop there.

Since Colonial times, southern Maryland has been a tobacco-producing area. At the small Hallowing Point Park, a 150-year-old tobacco barn is representative of the many antebellum barns that dotted the landscape. A sign explains the barn's history as well as the process of tobacco farming.

A pleasant and unexpected find in these parts is the Battle Creek Cypress Swamp Sanctuary, owned by The Nature Conservancy. The sanctuary sits at the northernmost limits for bald cypress trees in the United States. On a boardwalk trail through a tall canopy of trees and cypress knees that protrude from the still, black water, the peaceful silence is broken only by the melodious tunes of songbirds or the occasional croaking frog.

The Jefferson Patterson Park and Museum, located on the shores of the Patuxent River, has exhibits that trace twelve thousand years of the area's history. The park boasts a gallery, museum, farm exhibit building, archeological sites, and trails through its 560-acre site. During the War of 1812, the largest naval battle in Maryland's history took place here at the Battle of St. Leonard Creek.

While exploring the historical attractions of southern Maryland, you will also find abundant opportunities to enjoy the beauty of the Chesapeake Bay. The Flag Ponds Nature Park offers hiking trails, a wetland boardwalk, a fishing pier, and beach and picnic facilities, while nearby Calvert Cliffs State Park brings you up close to the majestic bluffs that line some thirty miles of the Chesapeake's western shoreline. These cliffs, which formed over fifteen million years ago when a warm and shallow sea covered southern Maryland, contain more than six hundred species of fossils, including shark's teeth and mollusk shells. Fossil collecting (at its best after a storm) is allowed at the park. The beach is reached via a two-mile hike.

The highlight of this trip is the historic maritime community of Solomons Island, located at the southern tip of Calvert County where the Patuxent flows into the bay. Solomons became an important oyster harvesting and processing center when Isaac Solomon opened a cannery here in 1870. At the same time, a shipbuilding and repair industry emerged to service the fishing vessels. By the end of the century, the small channel that separated the island from the mainland had been filled in with discarded oyster shells, which made it hard to distinguish where the mainland ended and the island began.

After the turn of the century, oyster harvests declined, watermen left the area, and the remaining boatyards turned from workboats to pleasure boats. Today, Solomons is primarily a tourist town. It offers charter fishing and recreational boating from its busy marinas, as well as a wide selection of lodging and seafood restaurants. The centerpiece of the little town's waterfront is the picturesque Drum Point Lighthouse. The screw-pile lighthouse was decommissioned in 1962 and moved here in 1975 to be part of the excellent Calvert Marine Museum.

For the final stop on the trip, leave Calvert County and travel across the Thomas Johnson Memorial Bridge into St. Mary's County. Pay a visit to Sotterley Plantation, an eighteenth-century tobacco plantation that is located on the western shore of the Patuxent. Pleasant hours can be spent touring the uniquely constructed manor house, the earliest section of which was built in the early 1700s, and its beautiful eighteenth-century garden. An interpretive walking trail traverses the scenic grounds and stops at several plantation dependencies, including a slave cabin.

PART VI

WASHINGTON SLEPT HERE

ABOVE: *As the sun rises over the Potomac River, it lights up the manor house at George Washington's Mount Vernon Estate.*

FACING PAGE: *An excellent view of the famous Horsehead Cliffs can be found at Fossil Beach in Westmoreland State Park.*

An exploration of northeastern Virginia reveals an area that is defined largely by the Potomac River. After tumbling over the Fall Line northwest of Washington, D.C., the great river flows through the nation's capital and heads southeast, toward its rendezvous with the Chesapeake Bay. Along the way, it serves as Virginia's border with southern Maryland.

A rich legacy of colonial history can be found here, along the banks of the Potomac. Wealthy and prominent Virginians, including several Revolutionary patriots, established large plantations along the river's shores south of Washington, D.C. The most notable of those plantation owners was the father of our country, George Washington. The trips in this chapter visit many sites related to the first president, including his birthplace on the Potomac, the Fredericksburg farm where he spent much of his childhood, and his beloved Mount Vernon estate, where he spent most of his adult life and is his final resting place.

Numerous parks and nature experiences also can be found throughout the region. Wildlife refuges along the Potomac serve to protect the local bald eagle population.

On a journey to the quiet and rural countryside of Virginia's Northern Neck, you'll visit farms, wineries, and Potomac parks, as well as the birthplace of Confederate General Robert E. Lee. The Fredericksburg area features other sites relating to the Civil War, including the Fredericksburg and Spotsylvania National Military Park, which provides a fascinating study of the events that befell this strategically important area during that brutal war.

THE NORTHERN NECK

ROUTE 23

From Virginia Route 3 in Oak Grove, take Virginia Secondary Route 638 (Leedstown Road) south to Ingleside Plantation Vineyards. Continue south on Route 638 and turn right on Virginia Secondary Route 637 (Layton Landing Road) to Westmoreland Berry Farm at Berry Farm Lane. From the farm, continue north on Route 637 (Rappahannock Road), and turn right on Virginia Secondary Route 634 (Claymont Road) to Route 3. Turn right and follow Route 3 east to a left turn on Virginia Route 204 and the George Washington Birthplace National Monument. Return to Route 3 and continue east. Turn left on Virginia Route 347 to Westmoreland State Park. Backtrack and turn left on Route 3, then turn left on Virginia Route 214 to Stratford Hall. From Stratford Hall, continue on Route 3 to Montross.

Virginia's Northern Neck is a long, narrow peninsula that juts into the Chesapeake Bay and is nestled between the Potomac and Rappahannock Rivers. There are no big cities here—just small, quaint towns and historic villages. Watermen ply the rivers, bays, inlets, and creeks, while farmers tend to acres of corn, soybeans, and other crops. It is a quiet, unspoiled area that is teeming with rural charm.

This route explores the western half of the peninsula, an area with colonial history as rich as its soil. The drive begins at the town of Oak Grove (actually not much more than a crossroads), where a loop drive through farmland holds a few surprises. If you arrive here early in the morning, you may want to rearrange the itinerary and make this loop on your return trip, since the first stop is a winery!

Just a couple of miles south of Oak Grove, you will come upon Ingleside Plantation Vineyards, one of Virginia's oldest and largest wineries. You'll know you're getting close when you spot the vineyards that cover 70 acres of this 3,000-acre plantation.

The winery offers tours, tastings of its award-winning wines, a gift shop, and a small museum. As you exit the property, watch for the handsome plantation house on your left. Since its beginnings in 1834, the house has served as a boys' school, a Civil War garrison, and a courthouse.

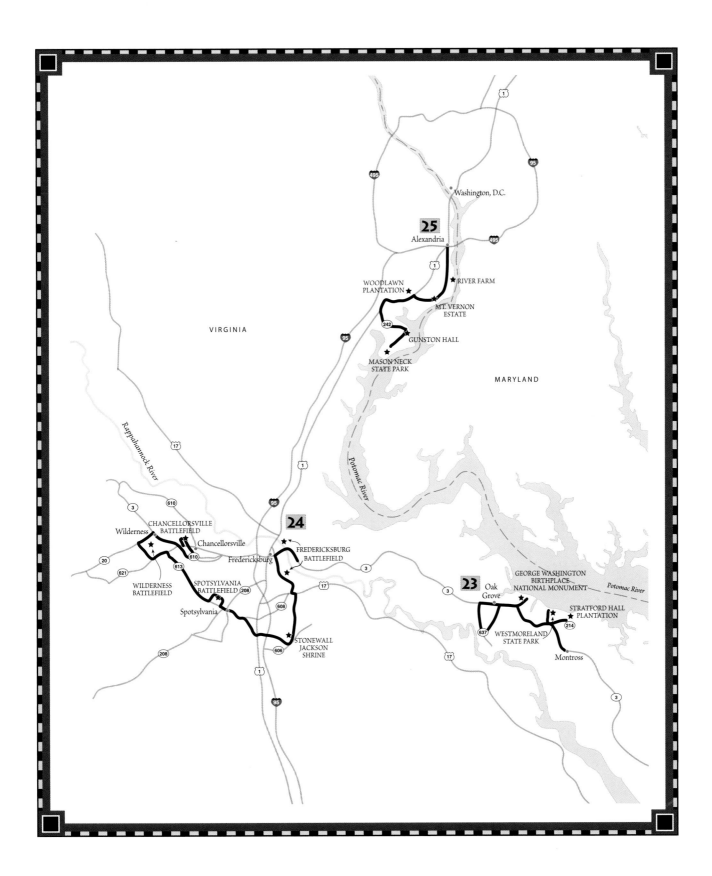

WOODLAWN
PLANTATION

★ RIVER FARM

MT. VERNON
ESTATE

25
Alexandria

Washington, D.C.

VIRGINIA

GUNSTON HALL

MASON NECK
STATE PARK

MARYLAND

Potomac River

Rappahannock River

CHANCELLORSVILLE
BATTLEFIELD

Wilderness

Chancellorsville

24

FREDERICKSBURG
BATTLEFIELD

Fredericksburg

WILDERNESS
BATTLEFIELD

SPOTSYLVANIA
BATTLEFIELD

Spotsylvania

STONEWALL
JACKSON
SHRINE

23 Oak
Grove

GEORGE WASHINGTON
BIRTHPLACE
NATIONAL MONUMENT

Potomac River

STRATFORD HALL
PLANTATION

WESTMORELAND
STATE PARK

Montross

LEFT: *A curious goat at the Westmoreland Berry Farm peers down from its overhead Goat Walk.*

BELOW: *Oyster shells mark the foundation of the original house at the George Washington Birthplace National Monument. The Memorial House and kitchen stand nearby.*

ABOVE: *Sheep graze in a meadow at the George Washington Birthplace National Monument.*

LEFT: *A detached kitchen near the Memorial House at the George Washington Birthplace National Monument is furnished with colonial cookware.*

A couple enjoys the horseback-riding trails and cabin accommodations at Westmoreland State Park, one of the six original state parks that opened in Virginia in 1936. Courtesy Virginia State Parks

Continue now to Westmoreland Berry Farm. This large farm is located on another former plantation that was first patented in 1641. During the Civil War, its plantation house was bombed and burned by Union gunboats. Today, Westmoreland offers a wide variety of seasonal berries on a pick-your-own basis or pre-picked in the Farm Market. They also have pre-picked apples, peaches, pumpkins, and other produce, as well as homemade jams, jellies, and pies.

For entertainment, you can watch the farm's adorable goats clamber around on an ingenious overhead goat walk. The sure-footed critters climb up a ramp from their goat pen to a narrow walkway that crosses over the farm road at twenty feet in the air. On the other end, there's a container that enchanted visitors can fill with goat chow and send up, via a pulley system, to the eager goats. It's great fun for adults, as well as kids (both the two-footed and four-footed variety).

Returning to Virginia Route 3, you'll pass back through Oak Grove en route to the next stop, the George Washington Birthplace National Monument. This farm, called Popes Creek Plantation, is where the father of our country came into this world on February 22, 1732. He lived there for the first three and a half years of his life. As a teenager studying surveying, George returned to the farm, then owned by his half-brother, and he continued to visit through 1771.

Crushed oyster shells mark the foundation of the original house, which burned on Christmas Day of 1779. A Memorial House was constructed in 1931. It was not intended to be an exact replica of the original, but a representation of a typical 1730s dwelling for a planter of moderate wealth, which depicts the culture and social standing of the Washington family.

The farm spreads out along Popes Creek, a tributary of the Potomac. Heritage livestock, typical of the Colonial era, inhabit the fields, pens, and barns. A road accesses the Washington family burial ground and continues down to a beach on the Potomac. A quiet picnic ground and nature trail are also available.

The next stop is Westmoreland State Park, one of the six original Virginia state parks that opened in June of 1936. This beautiful park encompasses 1,299 acres that stretch for 1.5 miles along the Potomac. It offers campgrounds, cabins, a swimming pool, fishing, boating, hiking, and picnicking. Another favorite activity is searching along Fossil Beach for remains of ancient marine mammals from the Miocene Sea. Fossils, shells, sharks' teeth, and whalebones are frequently found along the beach, where they are exposed by the erosion of the park's famous Horsehead Cliffs.

Just past the park is the turnoff for Stratford Hall Plantation, home to the powerful Lee family and birthplace of its most famous member, General Robert E. Lee.

Thomas Lee, who was a member of the governing council of the colony and acting governor of Virginia, purchased the 1,500-acre plantation in 1717 and completed its "Great House" in 1738. The magnificent brick Georgian mansion and its dependencies sit atop high bluffs overlooking the Potomac.

Thomas and his wife, Hannah, had six sons and two daughters. Two of the sons were signers of the Declaration of Independence. The oldest son, Philip Ludwell Lee, inherited Stratford Hall. Philip, in turn, willed it to his daughter, the "divine Matilda." She married her second cousin, the dashing Revolutionary War hero Henry "Light Horse Harry" Lee, who was left a life estate in the plantation when Matilda died in 1790. He later married Anne Hill Carter, who gave birth to a son, Robert Edward Lee, on January 19, 1807.

Robert lived fewer than four years at Stratford Hall. When Robert was just a toddler, his father was carted off to debtor's prison after his fortunes had declined due to bad land speculation. When he was released, the family moved to Alexandria, where they led a modest life. Henry's oldest son, Henry IV, became the master of Stratford Hall, and Robert made frequent visits over the years.

In 1929, the Robert E. Lee Memorial Association, a nonprofit organization, purchased the plantation and meticulously restored it. A visit includes a guided house tour and a self-guided tour of the spacious grounds, gardens, dependencies, and reconstructed gristmill. There are hiking trails and stunning views of the Potomac, as well as a restaurant that serves fabulous crab cakes!

The journey terminates in Montross, the county seat of Westmoreland County. The county courthouse was built in 1707, and it holds some of the oldest historic records in America. The little town has a museum, restaurants, and a country inn.

THE RELENTLESS CONFLICT

Location has played a vital role in the history of Fredericksburg, Virginia. In fact, the town's very existence can be attributed to its location. Nestled in a crook of the Rappahannock River, just below the fall line, the town was established in 1728 as a river port, in what was then the Virginia frontier.

During the Civil War, Fredericksburg's location again played a major role, this time to disastrous results. Situated midway between the Union capital of Washington, D.C., and the Confederate capital of Richmond, Fredericksburg and the surrounding counties were literally in the line of fire.

The first part of this trip focuses on the area's Civil War involvement. The Fredericksburg and Spotsylvania National Military Park encompasses the battlefields of Fredericksburg, Chancellorsville, Wilderness, and Spotsylvania Court House. These four major engagements of the Civil War occurred within a seventeen-mile radius, claimed more than one hundred thousand casualties, and left much of the area devastated. The park's exhibits, monuments, trails, and educational programs help visitors to understand the events that took place. Visitors' centers are located at Fredericksburg and Chancellorsville, while Wilderness and Spotsylvania contain exhibit shelters.

ROUTE 24

Begin at Fredericksburg Battlefield Visitor Center on Lafayette Boulevard and pick up a copy of the brochure "Touring the Battlefields." Tour Fredericksburg Battlefield. From Fredericksburg, head west on Virginia Route 3 and stop at Chancellorsville Battlefield Visitor Center. Turn right on Bullock Road, then right on Route 610 (Elys Ford Road). Stay on Route 610 (it becomes Old Plank Road) to a right turn on Furnace Road. Turn right on Sickles Drive, bear left on Stuart Drive, and return to Route 3. Turn left on Route 3, then left on Virginia Route 20 (Constitution Highway). Turn left on Hill-Ewell Drive to enter Wilderness Battlefield. Turn left on Route 621 (Orange Plank Road), then right on Route 613 (Brock Road). Turn right on unpaved Jackson Trail West, and at the end, turn right on Route 613. Go left on Grant Drive to Spotsylvania Battlefield. From the battlefield, turn right on Virginia Route 208 (Courthouse Road), then left on Route 608 (Massaponax Church Road). Turn right on U.S. Highway 1, then left on Route 607 (Guinea Station Road). Turn left on Route 606 (Stonewall Jackson Road) to visit Stonewall Jackson Shrine. From the shrine, turn left on Route 606, and then left on Route 609 to U.S. Highway 17. Turn left on U.S. 17, right on Route 608 (Benchmark Road), left on Mine Road, and right on Route 638 to Fredericksburg Battlefield. Return to Fredericksburg and explore the Old Town district. Take Williams Street (Route 3) to Chatham Manor, and continue south on Route 3 to Ferry Farm.

ABOVE: *Cannons stand behind the old Confederate breastworks atop Prospect Hill at the Fredericksburg Battlefield.*

OPPOSITE, TOP: *A marker in the Lacy family cemetery at Ellwood Plantation identifies the burial site of Stonewall Jackson's amputated arm.*

OPPOSITE, BOTTOM: *During the annual Memorial Day weekend Luminaria in the Fredericksburg National Cemetery, 15,300 candles are lit to represent the number of U.S. soldiers buried there.*

ARM OF
STONEWALL JACKSON
MAY 3, 1863.
___

The Confederate victory at the Battle of Fredericksburg is depicted in this Currier and Ives lithograph. The battle was considered to be General Robert E. Lee's easiest victory. Courtesy Library of Congress, Prints & Photographs Division

Starting at the Fredericksburg Battlefield Visitor Center, obtain the battlefield auto tour map and then proceed to the other battlefields in chronological order. Virginia Route 3, from Fredericksburg to Chancellorsville, is congested and heavily developed; unfortunately, it is the only logical route. By the time you reach Chancellorsville, the traffic and congestion is greatly reduced. The remainder of the journey is mostly a pleasant drive through peaceful woods and countryside.

The Battle of Fredericksburg occurred on December 11–13, 1862, when Ambrose Burnside and his Union forces, on their way to Richmond, met and battled with Robert E. Lee's Confederate Army in Fredericksburg. The Confederates successfully drove the Union troops back across the Rappahannock and earned Lee his easiest victory.

After touring the Fredericksburg Battlefield (except for Chatham Manor, which you will visit later), continue on to Chancellorsville, where another major battle raged from April 27 to May 6, 1863. Through brilliant military maneuvering, Lee secured his greatest victory at Chancellorsville. But, his victory was marred by tragedy when his most valued and trusted subordinate, Thomas "Stonewall" Jackson, was mistakenly shot by his own troops.

The Battle of the Wilderness (May 5–6, 1864) marked the first encounter between Lee and Ulysses S. Grant. After two days of fighting that resulted in heavy casualties on both sides, the battle ended in a draw. Grant began pulling out on May 7, but then engaged Lee farther south at Spotsylvania Court House. (To visit Ellwood Manor at the Wilderness Battlefield, be sure to obtain a pass at the Chancellorsville Battlefield Visitors Center.)

A series of engagements were fought during the bloody two-week Battle of Spotsylvania Court House (May 8–21, 1864), where casualties totaled nearly thirty thousand. On May 12–13, twenty continuous hours of the most intense hand-to-hand conflict of the war took place at the "Bloody Angle." At the end of two weeks, Grant disengaged and pushed on to Richmond.

Near the Spotsylvania Courthouse, turn onto Virginia Secondary Route 608, which is also known as the Route of Jackson's Ambulance. It leads to the Stonewall Jackson Shrine at Guinea Station and the site of Jackson's death. Jackson was brought to this plantation outbuilding after he was wounded at the Battle of Chancellorsville.

Return to Fredericksburg along country backroads and re-enter the city through the back of the battlefield. At the Fredericksburg Visitors Center, on Caroline Street in Old Town, pick up a tour map. The map identifies the city's historic sites, including a number of Colonial era sites linked to George Washington. After exploring the sites related to the city of yesteryear, you may want to take time to enjoy twenty-first-century Fredericksburg. It is a vibrant city with an excellent array of fine shops, galleries, and restaurants.

Several sites of particular interest are located in Old Town. The Old Masonic Lodge No. 4 is where George Washington became a mason in 1752. At the Hugh Mercer Apothecary Shop, Dr. Mercer treated patients (probably including his friend, George Washington) for fifteen years, with remedies like coltsfoot, saffron, and live leeches. Charles Washington, George's younger brother, built a home on Caroline Street in about 1760. In 1792, Charles' home was converted into a tavern and stagecoach stop, The Rising Sun Tavern. George Washington's sister, Betty, and her husband, Fielding Lewis, a prominent planter and merchant, built Kenmore in the mid-1700s. Kenmore was one of the most elegant houses in America. Just a few blocks away is the Mary Washington House. In 1772, George Washington bought this house for his mother so that she could be near her daughter. Mary lived here the last fifteen years of her life.

THE DEATH OF "STONEWALL"

With the exception of General Robert E. Lee, no commander was more honored and revered by Southerners than the legendary General Thomas J. "Stonewall" Jackson.

Jackson earned his famous nickname at the Battle of First Manassas (Bull Run). As Confederate forces were crumbling under Union fire, Jackson's brigade held its ground. Seeing this, Brigadier General Barnard E. Bee cried to his troops, "There stands Jackson like a stone wall. Rally behind the Virginians!" The Confederates went on to win that battle, and Jackson's nickname stuck.

Jackson was indispensable to Lee. He earned major Confederate victories during the Shenandoah Valley Campaign, before joining up with Lee for later battles. The two brilliant military men performed superbly together and achieved important victories at Fredericksburg and Chancellorsville. It was at Chancellorsville, however, that Lee lost his friend and most valuable commander.

After the victorious battle, on May 2, 1863, Jackson was returning to camp with staff members when they were mistaken for the enemy and fired on by members of the 18th North Carolina Infantry. Two bullets struck his left arm, which was later amputated at a field hospital near Wilderness Tavern. His chaplain, B. Tucker Lacy, took the severed arm to his brother's nearby farm, Ellwood, and buried it in the Lacy family cemetery. A simple monument marks the grave at Ellwood, which is now a part of the Fredericksburg and Spotsylvania National Military Park and open to the public at varying times (inquire at the visitors' center).

On May 4, Jackson was moved to a plantation outbuilding, some thirty miles from the battlefield, to recuperate. He contracted pneumonia and could not recover. On May 10, 1863, with his wife by his side, Stonewall Jackson died at the age of thirty-nine. Calling out in delirium, his last words were, "Let us cross over the river and rest under the shade of the trees."

He was buried on May 15 in Lexington, Virginia, where he had lived the last ten years before the war and worked as a professor at Virginia Military Institute. Over the years, attempts have been made to reunite Jackson with his arm, but so far they remain separated.

Legendary Confederate General Thomas "Stonewall" Jackson was most renowned for his Shenandoah Valley Campaign of 1862. Courtesy Library of Congress, Prints & Photographs Division

OPPOSITE PAGE: *Spring wildflowers and blooming redbud trees pretty a roadside within the Fredericksburg and Spotsylvania National Military Park.*

RIGHT: *Dancers in colonial attire entertain during a festival at Ferry Farm in Fredericksburg, the boyhood home of George Washington.*

BELOW: *From the piazza of his Mount Vernon estate, George Washington enjoyed an expansive view of the Potomac River.*

Drive across the Rappahannock River on Williams Street (Virginia Route 3) to visit Chatham Manor, which is a part of the Fredericksburg Battlefield. Built around 1770, the Georgian-style mansion was once the center of a large plantation. During the Battle of Fredericksburg, it served as both a Union headquarters and a field hospital.

End your trip at Ferry Farm, the boyhood home of George Washington. He lived on the 600-acre farm, on the east bank of the Rappahannock, from the age of six until he was twenty years old. This is where he received his formal education and where he learned to survey. It is also the site where young George allegedly chopped down the cherry tree and threw the coin (actually, it was a stone) across the river.

George inherited the farm when his father died in 1743. Nine years later, his half-brother Lawrence died and left him Mount Vernon. George moved, and his mother managed Ferry Farm for twenty-nine years. In 1772, he moved her to the house in town and sold the farm to Hugh Mercer.

No Washington family structures remain at Ferry Farm, but archeological excavations are underway to find their locations. A walking tour map, available from the visitors' center, identifies interesting sites such as the old ferry landing that gave the farm its name.

POTOMAC PLANTATIONS AND PARKS

ROUTE 25

From Alexandria, follow George Washington Memorial Parkway south. Take a left off of the parkway to access East Boulevard Drive and River Farm (American Horticultural Society). Return to the parkway and continue south to Mount Vernon Estate and Gardens. From Mount Vernon, proceed south on Virginia Route 235 (Mount Vernon Memorial Highway) to Washington's Gristmill, and then on to Woodlawn Plantation at the intersection of Route 235 and U.S. Highway 1. From Woodlawn, head south on U.S. 1. Turn left on Virginia Route 242 (Gunston Road) to Gunston Hall. Continue east on Route 242 and turn right on High Point Road to visit Mason Neck State Park.

South of Washington, D.C., along the banks of the Potomac River, wealthy Virginia gentlemen established magnificent colonial plantations. Many of these plantations have been preserved, restored, and opened to the public. This excursion visits those grand estates, as well as parks and wildlife refuges on the Potomac.

Begin your travels on the scenic George Washington Memorial Parkway, south of Alexandria, and make your first stop at River Farm, which is part of a 1,800-acre property once owned by George Washington. He purchased the farm in 1760 from William Clifton, who operated an inn and public ferry at what was then called "Clifton's Neck." Washington never lived at River Farm, which was the northernmost of the five farms that made up his Mount Vernon Plantation.

The farm remained in the Washington family until 1859, when it was split up and sold in pieces. In 1919, the part of the property that included present-day River Farm was sold to Malcolm Matheson. Matheson transformed his twenty-seven-acre farm (by then called Wellington) into a stunning country estate and completely reconstructed the original 1757 house. Outdoors, he planted boxwood, magnolia, wisteria, and other ornamentals to create a park-like setting.

When the property went on the market in 1971, the American Horticultural Society acquired it through the generosity of a board member. The society agreed to keep it open "for the enjoyment of the American people." Renaming it River Farm, the A.H.S. moved its headquarters here in 1973. As you would expect, the society maintains the beautiful grounds with a variety of gardens and groves to wander through and a lovely view of the Potomac.

Your next stop is the most notable of Virginia's, if not the entire nation's, historic homes. This is where the father of our country lived with his wife, Martha, from the time of their marriage in 1759, until his death in 1799.

Mount Vernon included 2,000 acres when Washington inherited it in 1761. Over the years, he purchased much of the surrounding land and expanded the estate to 8,000 acres. The plantation was divided into five separate farms and each had its own overseer, buildings, and work force. The farm where he and his family lived was called the "Mansion House Farm." He expanded the mansion from its original six rooms to twenty-one rooms.

Washington loved to be at Mount Vernon. He humbly stated that his most important occupation was that of a farmer. Though he longed to lead a quiet farming life at Mount Vernon, he was called to lead an emerging nation through a revolution and into its first steps of democracy. He finally retired to Mount Vernon in 1797, but he died there two short years later from a throat infection at the age of sixty-seven.

George Washington spent the final years of his life at his beloved Mount Vernon and its sprawling grounds. Courtesy Library of Congress, Prints & Photographs Division

In 1858, the Mount Vernon Ladies Association purchased the deteriorating property from the Washington family, and opened it to the public in 1860. Today, you can tour the mansion, a dozen outbuildings, and four gardens, plus the Ford Orientation Center and the Donald W. Reynolds Museum and Education Center. All are guaranteed to enlighten you on the private, as well as the public, life of this fascinating man. Three miles from the main estate, you'll find Washington's Gristmill, a carefully reconstructed, working replica of the one that occupied this site in the eighteenth century.

Before he died, George Washington gave 2,000 acres of his Mount Vernon estate to his nephew, Major Lawrence Lewis, and his bride, Eleanor Parke Custis, Martha Washington's granddaughter, as a wedding gift. William Thornton, a prominent architect and the first architect of the U.S. Capitol in Washington, D.C., was hired by Lewis to design their elegant brick Georgian mansion. The Woodlawn Plantation was completed in 1805. In 1952, the property was the first historic site to be acquired by the newly created National Trust for Historic Preservation.

Also located on the property is the Pope-Leighey House. Designed by noted architect Frank Lloyd Wright, the modest, contemporary house was built in 1941 for a Northern Virginia journalist named Pope and then sold to the Leighey family. With his "Usonian" design, Wright responded to the need for attractive, functional, and affordable housing for the middle class. The house was donated to the National Trust in 1964 and moved from its original site in Falls Church.

The remaining stops of the trip are located on Mason Neck, a peninsula that is surrounded by the waters of Pohick Bay on the north, Belmont Bay on the south, and the Potomac River on the east.

OPPOSITE PAGE: *A boardwalk trail along the Potomac River meanders through Mason Neck State Park.*

RIGHT: *Gunston Hall was the plantation home of founding father and author of Virginia's Declaration of Rights, George Mason.*

BELOW: *In addition to the manor house, Gunston Hall Plantation includes reconstructed outbuildings, a 250-year-old boxwood garden, and a marvelous view of the Potomac.*

Gunston Hall was the 5,500-acre plantation of one of the most influential, but lesser known patriots, George Mason. Mason was a private man who despised politics; he preferred to influence the course of history through his writings and discussions with friends. In May 1776, he penned Virginia's Declaration of Rights, in which he declared such inherent natural rights as "the enjoyment of life and liberty" and "pursueing and obtaining happiness and safety." Shortly thereafter, similar wording appeared in the Declaration of Independence, which was authored by his friend Thomas Jefferson. Later, Mason's Declaration of Rights became the basis for the U.S. Constitution's Bill of Rights.

Completed in 1759, Mason's lovely Georgian mansion features exquisite interior woodwork and carvings. The 550-acre site includes reconstructed outbuildings, a 250-year-old boxwood garden, and a half-mile trail to the Potomac.

Mason Neck National Wildlife Refuge, Mason Neck State Park, the Northern Virginia Park Authority, Gunston Hall Plantation, and the Virginia Department of Game and Inland Fisheries all work together in the management of over 5,600 acres on Mason Neck in an effort to provide recreational activities and, at the same time, protect the area's natural resources.

In the 1800s and early 1900s, Mason Neck's American bald eagle population rapidly declined, due to a combination of the stripping of mature pine and hardwood trees by the logging industry and the use of the pesticide DDT. In 1969, Mason Neck National Wildlife Refuge became the first refuge established specifically to protect the bald eagle. The refuge is accessed by hiking trails and contains 2,000 acres of hardwood forest, Northern Virginia's largest freshwater marsh, and 4.4 miles of shoreline. It supports a diversity of wildlife, and it has the largest blue heron rookery in the Mid-Atlantic.

Mason Neck State Park offers hiking trails, picnic areas, interpretive programs, and a launch for canoes and kayaks. In addition to bald eagles, the park is also a place to see two hundred other bird species, white-tailed deer, fox, and beavers. The park has a shared entrance with the refuge.

In its pleasant bayside setting, the Pohick Bay Regional Park offers camping, cabin rentals, boating, fishing, nature trails, bridle paths, picnic facilities, and an eighteen-hole golf course.

SUGGESTED READING

Colbert, Judy. *Virginia: Off The Beaten Path.* 9th ed. Guilford, Conn.: Globe Pequot Press, 2006.

Maryland and Delaware Atlas & Gazetteer. 4th ed. Yarmouth, Maine: DeLorme Publishing, 2000.

Miller, Joanne. *Moon Handbooks: Maryland & Delaware.* 2nd ed. Emeryville, Calif.: Avalon Travel Publishing, 2004.

Miller, Joanne. *Moon Handbooks: Pennsylvania.* 3rd ed. Emeryville, Calif.: Avalon Travel Publishing, 2005.

Pennsylvania Atlas & Gazetteer. 6th ed. Yarmouth, Maine: DeLorme Publishing, 2000.

Ross, John. *The Atlantic Coast & Blue Ridge: The Smithsonian Guides to Natural America.* New York: Random House Publishing, Washington, D.C.: Smithsonian Books, 1995.

Seldon, Lynn. *Country Roads of Maryland and Delaware.* 2nd ed. Lincolnwood, Ill.: Country Roads Press, 1999.

Seldon, Lynn. *Country Roads of Virginia.* 2nd ed. Lincolnwood, Ill.: Country Roads Press, 1999.

Seldon, Lynn. *Country Roads of West Virginia.* 1st ed. Lincolnwood, Ill.: Country Roads Press, 1999.

Smith, Julian. *Moon Handbooks: Virginia.* 3rd ed. Emeryville, Calif.: Avalon Travel Publishing, 2005.

Virginia Atlas & Gazetteer. 4th ed. Yarmouth, Maine: DeLorme Publishing, 2000.

West Virginia Atlas & Gazetteer. 1st ed. Yarmouth, Maine: DeLorme Publishing, 1997.

INDEX